THE STRUCTURE OF CONSCIOUSNESS

This publication is designed to provide accurate and authoritative information regarding the subject matter covered. While the publisher and author have used their best efforts in preparing this book, they make no representations or warranties with respect to the accuracy or completeness of the contents of this book and specifically disclaim any implied warranties of merchantability or fitness for a particular purpose. The advice and strategies contained herein may not be suitable for your situation. You should consult with a professional when appropriate. Neither the publisher nor the author shall be liable for any loss of profit or any other commercial damages, including but not limited to special, incidental, consequential, personal, or other damages.

No portion of this book may be reproduced in any form without written permission from the publisher or author, except as permitted by U.S. copyright law.
Established—April 2024-Feburary 2025

New York, NY
United States of America
© 2025 Baruch Menache
All rights reserved.
Published by McWest & Associates
ISBN: 978-1-971928-22-7

www.ingramcontent.com/pod-product-compliance
Lightning Source LLC
LaVergne TN
LVHW012042070526
838202LV00056B/5558

THE STRUCTURE OF CONSCIOUSNESS

Baruch Menache

Part I: Foundations of Structural Consciousness 1

Consciousness: Structural Foundations 3

The Exchange between Structural Environments and Sociality 5
The Approaches to Consciousness and Consequences 9
The Dynamics of Consciousness Exchange and Systemic Stability 11

The Dynamics of Consciousness and Contextual Regulation 15

The Structure of Consciousness and Renunciation 19

Part II: Recreated Reality and Conceptual Mediation............... 23

The Recreated Structural Reality...................... 25

The First Side of Recreation: Immediate Separation 25
Gaining Consciousness through Arbitrary Means 26
Altruism and Structural Service...27
Departure from Consciousness and Return to Structural Reality 27
Altruism and the Stranger: Recreated vs. Structural Reality 28
Biological Necessities and Structural Reality...29
Seeking Convergence between Structural and Recreated Reality 30
The Outcome: Consciousness Overlays Structural Reality 31
Architectural Feats and Functional Limitations..35

Consciousness, Context, and the Perceptual Psyche 37

Choosing Context: Navigating Forced and Voluntary Interactivity 40
Navigating Internal Autonomy and Perceptual Exposure.........................41
Perceptual vs. Internal Interaction 48
Social Buffers & Higher-Order Mediation 51
Separation in Conflict & Trauma Processing 52

Part III: Redundancy, Multiplicity & Representational Loops 53

Redundancy and Access: The Psychosocial Logic of Imitation 55
Individual and Collective Choices in Shaping Redundancy 57

The Interplay of Zero & Redundancy in Existential Systems 59
Self-Consciousness and the Cycle of Multiplicity 62
Redundancy and its Role in Multiplicity 63

Representational and Genuine Systems of Consciousness 65

Structural & Conceptual in Psychological Experience 69

Representation, Interaction, and Physicality 75

Consciousness as a Reflective Mode 79
The Regulation of Psyche through Conscious Interaction 81
Interaction with Representational Figures 83
The Perpetual Loop of Representational Interaction 86
Binary Requirement of Representational Interaction 88

Part IV: Cosmic, Political & Systemic Locale 93

Cosmic Elements: Local Interaction and Social Agreement 95

Celestial Adaptability and Individual Experience 96
Cosmic Balance and Conceptual Interaction 97
Domestication and Reality 99
The Central Locale and Universal Interaction 101

Two Lineages of Consciousness 105

Localized and Universal Consciousness 106

Corporeal and Conceptual Consciousness 109

Corporeal Representation in Consciousness 110
Between Conceptual and Corporeal Consciousness 110
Balancing Consciousness: The Need for Integration 111
Consciousness, Memory, and Systemic Integration 114
The Stagnation of Memory-Based Relationships and Consciousness 116

Consciousness, Social Exchange, and the Continuum 119

Dependencies, Growth, and Evolutionary Interactions 123

Cosmic Influences and Political Systems 126

The Political System and the Centric Locale 129

Internal Dynamics 129
External Dynamics 134

Part V: Celebration, Trauma, and Encapsulation 141

Celebration in Structuring Time and Memory .. 143

Memory, Experience, and the Nature of Consciousness 144
Dynamics and the Necessity of Temporal Distinctions in Consciousness
.... 144
The Psyche and Extended Interaction.. 145
The Limits of Simulation.. 146
Categorization and Encapsulation in Celebrations and Trauma 147
The Makeup of Celebrations and Trauma 147
Intimacy and Ritual 148

The Convergence of Consciousness and the Holiday Experience 149

The Risk of Mischaracterization in Celebration 150
Encapsulation and Traumatic Exposure 151
The Nature of Encapsulation 151
Categorization and the Loss of Encapsulation... 152
The Vulnerabilities of Continuous Encapsulation 153
Encapsulation and Contrast 155

Part VI: Integration, Collapse, and the Edge of Conscious Systems 157

The Interaction between Structure and Streamline Consciousness 159

The Slow Infusion: How Consciousness Becomes Structured Reality ... 162
Activation vs. Convergence: When Reality Misses Itself 165
Consciousness in Retreat and Social Disintegration 166
Celebration and the Conscious System 169

Consciousness and Existential Instability: A Comparative Analysis 175

The United States: Consciousness Enmeshed 176
Russia: Existential Instability and Detachment 176

The Interactive Foundations of Consciousness 179

The Interactive Mainframe and Consciousness 180

The Second Type of Interactive Locale: Exemplified Interactivity 183

Reconsidering the Separation of Space 187

Inconsistent Interactivity 189
The Encapsulation of Consciousness and Interactivity 191

PART I: FOUNDATIONS OF STRUCTURAL CONSCIOUSNESS

Consciousness: Structural Foundations[1]

Consciousness begins or commences based on a substrate of a depleted form of consciousness. That elementary modality is foundational because consciousness is structured as a hierarchy of degrees.

A single level of consciousness is reliant upon its elementary form to give it vitality. Because it is more complex, and complexity is not an available attribute for the retention of consciousness, whatever does not complete the complexity configuration becomes dependent upon an elementary form of consciousness.

That elementary module is in service and provides the provisions for the less complex aspects or the depleted end of that conscious spectrum so that the surpassing configuration of consciousness can experience a wholesome appearance. If we were to dismantle that service, the advanced

---

[1] In this discussion, several key terms will help clarify the dynamics of consciousness. *Consciousness peak* refers to the highest echelon of awareness within a hierarchical system, where complex interactions converge to form an elevated state of understanding. Supporting this structure is *subsidiary consciousness*, the foundational layers of awareness that provide essential input for more advanced forms. At the base of this hierarchy lies *lower-end consciousness*, the elemental aspects of awareness that serve as the building blocks for preeminent advanced states. This interplay relies on a process of *service*, wherein simpler forms of consciousness contribute to and sustain the development of more complex states. Central to this framework is *complexification*, the evolutionary process through which consciousness integrates diverse elements and interactions to create a spectrum of awareness.

The Structure of Consciousness

end of consciousness, or that of further complexity, would need to downgrade itself to provide for an experience of those attributes.

The reason those attributes are only available to a specific level of complexity that consciousness can attain is due to the platform limitation inherent in consciousness itself, as it is dependent on individuals and organisms for its expression.

For example, a building can imbue a certain degree of consciousness, and indeed it is only based on its platforming structure and rigid formation. The formation can display a sensibility to the direction of consciousness, but it cannot include all these complex developments that lead to that accomplishment. It is structurally bound to give only a single sequence of conscious experience, and the attributes that lead toward it must be neglected to achieve that goal, like the workers and construction. We could imagine a competent structure with the dystopia of all civilization to notice how it will lose its imbued consciousness and rather stand as itself, as the most simplistic formation of consciousness because no other provision has been selected for that. When we see a competent structure, we could always ask or analyze to find the lesser complexifications—what it is dependent upon to give it its impending level of consciousness.

A more concrete example would be the construction of a skyscraper devoid of a surrounding city or competent political entity. That final structure will not imbue a certain consciousness common with skyscrapers, but rather will take up the position of consciousness that does not have its dependence on civilization or a surrounding social body. Of course, we would notice that with the construction of the skyscraper, there will be a surrounding social body and prevalence of some sort of relevance in the hierarchy of conscious substance. However, that social body must be termed for its availability of consciousness in accordance with its structural origins and memory.

If we were to take an indigenous population and simply place them around the skyscraper, it would not imbue the skyscraper with a sensibility of consciousness as they would understand it, but rather, in much simpler terms, as being a structure to house, protect, and utilize—all the simplistic aspects that a structure provides. This is because this sociality is already in commencement of participation in another sociality that has developed its

Consciousness: Structural Foundations

complexification to that level, so that we almost perceive that skyscraper as a gateway to enter what is already known in their realm.

The Exchange between Structural Environments and Sociality

We may need to inquire about how the process of sociality ascertains its consciousness based on another sociality. If we were to follow the other sociality, why are they the advanced bearers of consciousness? This may be because the lower spectrum of consciousness and its service to the uppermost gradations retains a platform value for the advanced level of consciousness. This means that there is a constant renunciation between advanced and depleted levels of consciousness so that the advanced levels of consciousness are taking up the renunciation of the inferior ends for the obtainment and entertainment of that complexification, precluded and ameliorated with theirs. This is the service that is being performed by the inferior parts of consciousness, as they are providing a certain level of competency that, included with the emulation of the expected surpassing levels of consciousness, creates a wholesome formation.

That process of service can extend to social environments, to structural environments, to anything pertaining to consciousness, and to anything relevant to a conversation.

There is a sensibility that a social environment, which is in service to an elevated degree of sociality, might be redundant in its elemental state and replaceable because of the fact that it platforms a diminished level of complexification. With the level of competency at a deficient level, it is no surprise that there will be a multitude of availability amongst sociality to provide that substrate of consciousness. However, the competency of that service, the manner in which it platforms that complexification, and the exchange of values, are all part of the dynamic. For the purpose of the wholeness of consciousness, which can endeavor to be afforded to those who can prosper in the competency of their depleted-level consciousness. Even though there is redundancy in the multitude of that availability of service, this does not diminish the importance of enduring that process in an accompanying manner so that the sequential outcome is forthcoming. This is the hostility of the exchange of depleted and elevated levels of consciousness, in which it could be the case that there are even individuals who retain an advanced level of consciousness and thus are worthwhile to be in service to the peak of consciousness. However, because they have not understood the parameters of that exchange—where it can be done incompetently and incoherently—they are not included in the process.

We can understand this in a structural aspect, in which there are multitudes of contending structures or physical systems that can process the platform of this diminished level of complexification. Yet, there are certain communicational values or undefined elements that allow for a direct interaction with a specific structure, even as they do not retain a full formation of that necessary degree of complexification. The advanced structures are willing to surrender the perfect complexification required for their level, as long as it is direct and available for that exchange. Without the availability and communication between exchanges, it is lost to the possibility of any platform, and so it becomes a non-consequential element.

We can understand this by way of example: agriculture was a pre-history innovation that should have created a plethora of systems that would have extended intelligence between social beings. However, being that the communication element of writing was not part of their process, they were fairly limited to tradition and generational gaps. Even as the communication device cannot be attributed to the progress of civilization, it is those who used such a device that had the advantage despite the prevalent complexity of consciousness in the pre-historic era. Once the advent of writing became a part of systems, even a major gap such as the Dark Ages did not become lost in the civilized structure as noted in the Renaissance, which returned to ancient texts—communication elements that allowed for the exchange to continue unabated despite thousands of years of separation.

There is another possibility in which there is an exchange from structural environments to sociality that does not rely on other structural dependencies but rather on social dependencies. This would mean that instead of seeking out structural platforms of a less complex nature for the wholesome attainment of that current consciousness, it is upon the social environment to bring those understandings into this environment. In some way, it receives that recognition without ever having to stray away from its structural environment. This would require a high level of social interaction and diversity: with a depleted level of social interaction, it would not be the case that the environment retains a sensibility of its inferior forms; and without diversity, it will not be the case that the social environment understands environmental values that are external to the structure.

We observe a major shortcut underway in this possibility. Instead of structural environments relying on other structural environments, while sociality relies upon other sociality, they can both, in turn, purpose each other in a manner where neither has to seek out what is external to it. In the internal environment, whether social or structural, each will formulate the other to provide that external renunciation or subdued-level consciousness, so that somehow the city itself retains consciousness without ever noticing the controlled regulation and dependencies outside of that environment. If we follow our analysis, we can notice that this is, in part, based on the psychic material of the diverse crowd that is constantly propagating within these environments, bringing in external formations, while the structural environment provides other external formations based on other sociality that has been previously introduced. It becomes a cyclical internality where the sociality arrives with a depleted form of consciousness, and the structural environment recognizes the occasion and then sends it forth to other sociality and their internal space, unto which they succeed in structurally ascertaining a new value.

This occurs naturally in all structural environments, in which sociality ascertains its perception of that environment based on previous experiences and semblances of historical precedent. This is not an especially significant aspect of any environment, but it can be the case that it could be so developed that with diversity and interaction, the final product is a structural environment that is not dependent on external environments and is completely dependent on sociality itself. With this in place, the environment now retains a peak level of consciousness, with all that complexification accessible, allowing sociality to obtain that final exemplification that outweighs whatever previous semblance it has provoked.

Therefore, sociality functions as an exchange between society and its environment, wherein sociality represents a renunciation of its prior assemblages in favor of the current experience. This dynamic provides a structural environment that derives from previous models or exhibits diminished levels of complexification. Meanwhile, the environment offers the highest level of semblance, ensuring the possibility of interaction between the individual and this competent environment.

Metaphors serve as the unification of prior models. According to Lakoff and Johnson (1980), metaphors are not merely figurative but central to our everyday, embodied experiences, structuring our relationships and shaping everyday reality.[2]

As noted in Hannon, Riddle, and Ryberg (2014):

"Metaphorical work, therefore, structures our understanding and experiences of Internet communication in terms of movement, orientation, extension, and flows"…This metaphorical framework is crucial to prior assemblages. Hence, metaphors are more than just descriptive..."they are also productive and constitutive of the realities within learning environments. Additionally, they can be empirically traced within specific settings."[3]

However, when there is no interaction between the individual and an environment of such consciousness, they are providing a renunciation of semblance without the added provision of gaining entrance into that consciousness affair. There will be a consciousness influence, but it will be lost to the individual parameters because of a lack of interaction between them. Even more so, when we reach *peak consciousness* environments, it is fairly abstract to construct anything other than the imbued construct itself because it requires one to be constantly available in one's unique domain while interacting with that environment. That is a topic for another discussion, but it is still important to note at this juncture.

We saw the case is true of environments relying on sociality for their prior environments. We are going to question the case of sociality that relies on prior environments instead of prior sociality systems. This would mean that, instead of acquiescing to their dependencies upon inferior levels of sociality, they rely and depend upon weaker structural environments that provide that platform and nuance of consciousness.

We can imagine the case of an affluent individual—not in the sense of currency value, but rather in the domain structure of being affluent—so that they are part of a leadership in a conscious expansion that is more peak than the medium expansion. If this individual enters into substandard-level environments and structures, we could imagine they would obtain the understanding and influence of those complexifications so that they could continue on in their wholesome development. However, it is usually the case that they choose the other option, that of service, in which, through their currency nomination, they are able to economically order

---

[2] Lakoff, G., & Johnson, M. *Metaphors We Live By* (1980).

[3] Hannon, J., Riddle, M., & Ryberg, T., Assembling University Learning Technologies for an Open World (2014).

complexification to come to them. But because they are weary of the whole process, noting that they are unwilling to enter into these substandard environments, their exchange might not even occur through the service and would instead result in less activity and more being done by other people.

The manner in which a consciousness chooses its sacrificial representation with a weakened end of consciousness is based on a reduction method. If we were to remove that depleted end from the equation, we would observe the manner in which the larger complexification of consciousness continues. In the worst-case scenario, it would need to relinquish the platform of that complexification in order to succeed in the void of the substandard forms of consciousness.

It could be the case that consciousness continues unabated, even with the inclusion of that void, so that it espouses consciousness at a high level without the engineering of its foundational elements. If this occurs, then consciousness will exist with a vast degree of *shadow*-like material. These *shadow*s are the void of that complexification coupled with the unwillingness of the elevated-level consciousness to remove its stature. It would rather wait for the possibility of an elementary complexification to make its way into the system to fill that void and provision a workable system.

The Approaches to Consciousness and Consequences

The other option of regrouping and lowering its outlook is wearisome because it has a deeper understanding of consciousness, requiring to relinquish a degree of understanding, which is strenuous to perform. The two approaches are going to produce different results. The first, of remaining as it were with a stronger void, would present the possibility of upending the entire system without the possibility of regeneration. The void can become enlarged to a point where the corresponding reprocessing of the void would be less likely, and, more so, the skeletal system of consciousness would not be able to receive that data because it does not retain a perspective that can include more than its space. At an eventual moment, the consciousness would become so bare that it would not stabilize itself and would be unrelatable as a competent system, to which sociality does not adhere. This leads to the case of no return, for it cannot restructure itself, nor can the subsidiaries provide a nuance that would assist the system. This would require a collapse of the system.

The second approach—relinquishing the leaps of consciousness to preserve the stability of the void and to platform from those spaces—also

The Structure of Consciousness

comes with its drawbacks. While not at risk of a collapsible system, it creates the possibility of never returning to its former state and thus becoming a subsidiary for another consciousness sentiment to use for their stature. This is found in the process of aging, where there is an eventual admittance and commitment to the decline, followed by platforming from an elementary point in development, which can then be utilized by the current vitality of consciousness for stabilization and sociality. The other choice of aging would be the former, in which the decline of aging is perceived as an allowed premise of a void, to continue the development of consciousness. This is a based on a hope that the void would be filled, or finding and adhering to systems that would engender a maintenance of the underlining modalities of consciousness so that the decline of aging is not so. One can reach the conjecture of death with this approach intact, and this is usually the case for royal figures, who embody the choice of this approach—never appearing in decline but rather imbued with an esteem for growth in the midst of old age. The royal factions maintain, with a certain loyalty that goes beyond regular systems, the preservation of all the depleted platforms of consciousness.

The royal figure only needs to maintain a tip of that consciousness, with the rest assuming the role of care, so that there is no decline until the moment of death. This is only made possible because of the unnatural loyalty at play, existing only because there is unity under the political sphere of that royalty. Even with all those provisions, if there is a genuine decline, the representation of the royal figure is not enough to sustain this process unless they maintain the stature of consciousness. When they do not adhere to it, there is a perceived system that has not been actualized in real-time, for all are sacrificing their spectrum of consciousness for something that is bygone, thus making the whole system bygone. This is the risk of this approach, where even when the provisions that would usually account for the void are met by a loyal system, the consciousness peak that is not so will create an upending of the system from within.

By the very notion of loyalty, it will be the cause for an entire system that instantly becomes a fabrication, for none would adhere to it and provide for each other unless the consciousness peak is agreed. If it were in decline, the entire system would not know or be made aware, as well as the unwillingness to listen to the clear indications of such occurring. This would be the adverse effect of a non-normal dynamical exchange between the consciousness peak and the provisions for the underlining modality of consciousness, in which, surpassing the dynamical protection, it will have

Consciousness: Structural Foundations

no buffer, should the consciousness peak subside. The loyalty itself would be in complete decline, for there is no availability of reasserting a consciousness peak, as that agreement is only for consciousness itself, and not for the subsidiaries.

Remember, these subsidiaries are in complete renunciation for *peak consciousness*, so they do not dispel or disrupt the process but only enjoin to provide the pillars. The decline at the peak cannot be controlled or regulated by the subsidiaries and must be an internal process of mitigation within *peak consciousness* itself. The royal system has a buffer—that of political service—so that when the royal figure reaches a state of decline, the subservient of the system will simply move to another figure to represent the political system. Rome was very apt to this process and very willing to move from one head to another, adhering to the system for that allegiance rather than to the political head.

The Dynamics of Consciousness Exchange and Systemic Stability

We have a case where the system's inclination toward reduced complexity is the cause of upending the consciousness system. As well, we have the case of a *peak consciousness* that allows for the void, to a point where it becomes so skeletal that consciousness is unable to communicate or retrieve the missing parts, and thus reaches a true decline. We could even say that the latter, by choosing to participate only in a real dynamical exchange, places itself at the mercy of participants who are unwilling to surrender their meager consciousness by integrating it into the larger system. Of course, this is sensible, for just as the *peak consciousness* is unwilling to expand beyond its current limits, so do all the subordinate elements seek to retrieve their semblance of consciousness without having to give it over to another. This is only possible through the allowance and freedom of this dynamical exchange, which can be the cause of its misgivings.

For then we have autonomous agents of smaller consciousness, without their development on a spectrum or the purposeful engagement of their substance. We also have *peak consciousness* with an extreme void that has little renunciations as integrated into its system. We can consider such a circumstance to be termed 'pockets of consciousness', coexisting with *peak consciousness*, with neither having access to the other. The very hesitation of these pockets to offer their substance to the greater spectrum of consciousness is the cause of their stagnation. For by not being in communion with that, they have no way of maintaining or retaining it, and

The Structure of Consciousness

they become the void themselves. By hesitating to relinquish their little semblance of consciousness, they become part of the void—only as representations of that effect—and they will embody the experience of that void, with a greater resentment and hostility toward their position.

The void is rather a gap in consciousness, and the consciousness peak does not embody such an experience; rather, those who retain any sort of consciousness semblance that is not attached or given over to the system will become its gap. For how could they maintain consciousness outside the system without it being considered the horror of consciousness?

The interesting *thing* about this is that those pockets of consciousness consider the surrender of their individual consciousness to be a lapse and decline of their own system. However, it is the very notion of that position that is the cause of the decrepit nature they embody, for becoming the horror of consciousness is going to come at a cost to everything they endeavor. They presume that the renunciation of consciousness will be complete and this will result in the immediate decline of their participation, but the process is more complex than the non-sacrificial model they assume. Instead, it is the slow dynamical exchange between what they have to offer and what the system requests, and as they give over one substance, the interaction of this exchange will offer another. It is similar to a currency system, where continuous exchange—not merely the quantity of currency—creates value.

They will both give over the consciousness needed for the system and receive the exposure that is natural whenever interacting with that consciousness system. If we follow the train of thought, we would notice that those who embody the pockets of consciousness are doing so not because they believe that there is a complete renunciation waiting to occur but rather because they are unwilling to be exposed to more consciousness; rather to be content with whatever they retain.

This is a faulty premise in understanding consciousness, in which the retention of consciousness is assumed to be one's own or static. Consciousness of any substance is constantly mobile, vital, and alive to the current strands of the system, and the retention that one has is not an ownership but rather an exchange—similar to how a certain affluent perspective might believe that currency represents ownership and retention from the economic standard rather than an exchange that is worthless in its retention.

The inevitable complete renunciation of consciousness is only the semblance of the concurrence of the decline of life itself, a metaphorical perspective on existence in that sense. It is not self-sacrificial but rather an exchange where one reaches into a decline of life so that their exchange is less valued. It is not consciousness that is in decline or once an obtainment of consciousness, but rather the natural system of affairs in which individuals decline, develop, and process—and that will mirror the conscious exchange itself. When we notice that there seems to be a complete renunciation within a consciousness system, it is not the composite picture; rather, it is an individual who processes exchanges with consciousness, receives accordingly, and finally mirrors their decline within the conscious system instead of declining in seclusion.

This outlines certain parameters that are necessary for a continuous and perpetual conscious system:

[1] The retention of a dynamical exchange between *peak consciousness* and its subsidiaries, so that the dynamical exchange can serve as a buffer, ensuring that loyalty does not lead to the opening of the system when *peak consciousness* fails.

[2] The willingness to let go of that very buffer in the system of dynamical exchange, so that there's a compelling nature to the exchange which prevents individuals from falling into the freedom of their pockets of consciousness and becoming horrors of consciousness. As well, failing to provide what the system requires. In other words, the dynamic exchange should not be perfect, so that there is leeway for a process to endure without having to consider the philosophical mindsets for every individual and the mistakes in their placement into the horror of consciousness.

[3] *Peak consciousness* is willing to communicate and exchange with the pillars and the reduced complexifications of consciousness, so that even if the provision is being offered, it may immediately be declined by *peak consciousness*, for they assume an embodiment of the entire conscious system rather than its beacons.

[4] The consciousness peak is willing to endure a certain exposure to its gaps so that it does not adhere completely to the reduced complexity of that social system. When this occurs it will not be able to maintain the limited necessities and its relative *shadow* that endures in the natural state of affairs. In other words, it is willing to endure a certain degree of void to maintain the peak position.

[5] The notion of being self-aware, at least enough to recognize if it is necessary to relinquish the peak position and the platform, all at a reduced level of complexity, so as to maintain a semblance of position. This is

instead of facing the inevitable nature of a complete system decline. Of course, this is a choice that is only made when it is realized that the risk is too high for upending of the system. In this case, the re-platforming and positioning with a decline would occur without the consideration of bygone peak levels so that the entity can truly embody that depleted level and thus be available to serve as a leader for another peak. It can also be available to reiterate its position, that is, when it gains that embodiment and substance.

The Dynamics of Consciousness and Contextual Regulation

We can understand consciousness by way of analogy or, more so, through a framework that is prevalent for all individuals. There are specific times of day when the expansion of consciousness—or an individual's structural or other certainties—will be more prevalent, while at other times it will be less. The bright morning, for instance, is a scenario in which consciousness is confined to its encapsulated format.

This would mean that, upon studying the individual, although there is expansion, due to the prevalent contextual control and the morning space, consciousness does not have the ability to regulate and permeate as it normally would. Even those who relinquish contextual regulation in the morning—because both sociality and the biological state require certain functions that create contextual overlays—will experience the realization of expansion as encapsulated. The same is true for *structural consciousness*, which is also reliant on sociality for its existence, and thus will follow at the same proportion. Because the individual is of this kind, and their sociality and group function are similarly structured, the morning scenario will result in a consciousness that is subdued to an encapsulated format and

The Structure of Consciousness

abstract to perceive and extrapolate. Those who are more consciously prone—or locals who are more consciously prone—will be encapsulated but identifiable by their expansion when studied, and when the time comes for contextual detachment, consciousness will be exposed as it was.

At the individual level, consciousness will expose, but it will not gain access to the entire structure. Also, because there is no sincerity in the contextual attachments, one is in limbo between an illumination that does not subscribe to the entire psyche and a contextual realm that is not a choice but is rather permeable based on biological and social circumstances. Because of this disparity, consciously prone individuals will experience a certain frustrating sentiment, which, in terms of our analysis, is the disparity between contextual control and consciousness expansion. This is why it is commonplace for consciously prone individuals to partake in art forms that help mitigate the interactive structure of the psyche so that consciousness is allowed its proper expansion.

Additionally, on the contrary, consciously prone individuals may approach a direct lineage to conceptual overlay—not so much to become a contextualized individual but to fill the disparity between the expansion and the void. The same can be said for *structural consciousness*, in which a local who is consciously prone will endeavor either to partake in a mitigation of art forms or in contextual attention. Usually, the latter is the case, because when we discuss structural organization, due to its obscure nature, it has difficulty exhibiting art forms that will not undo the expansion and thus the process. In addition, all art form is individually prone, and making an attempt to form art through a diverse sociality is demanding to come by and potentially may have adverse effects. This is why it is more common to find *structural consciousness* adhering to an attention-prone contextual format—not due to inherent contextual construction, but to bridge the gap between potential and its inaccessibility within the morning happenstance.

For contextually prone individuals, the morning scenario aligns perfectly with their regulated consciousness. In fact, we could say from the outset that the process of their development is to attempt consciousness expansion at the very beginning, so as not to validate the contextual obsession, which will regulate the entirety of the day and thus preclude any consciousness exposure, relying instead on old themes and historical precedence. For them, art forms or other forms that gain entrance into the propagating factors of the psyche will not allow conscious discrimination through their system but rather become available to consciousness itself.

Aerts et al. (2000) grant a perspective on this concept, "Conceptual closure increases [contextuality] an order of magnitude further, by enabling the individual to engage in relational streams of thought that refine potential actions in light of goals or imagined outcomes. Thus the capacity to give evidence of consciousness is enhanced...The distributed storage and retrieval of memories prompt the emergence of abstractions, and as the density of abstractions increases, the probability they crystallize into an interconnected worldview increases exponentially. For this to happen, the sphere of concepts activated by any perturbation (that is, the extent to which storage/retrieval is distributed) must fall within an intermediate range; the system is poised at the proverbial 'edge of chaos'. A viable and coherent worldview is one that reinforces thought trajectories that enhance wellbeing at the individual and societal levels."[4]

There is a disparity in our objectives that arises from different approaches to art and consciousness. For those who are consciously attuned, art functions to complete an interactive process, allowing awareness to reach the deeper recesses of the psyche. In contrast, for those who respond to contextual cues, art serves as the entry point into a state of consciousness—until that moment, no interactive experience is available. In other words, art can either act as the gateway to consciousness or serve as a restorative mechanism that makes the mind more receptive. This dual role often leads to disappointment; if one assumes that art provides full access to consciousness when it is really only repairing isolated, previously closed-off aspects, they risk losing the progress they have already made, leading to further stagnation.

Similarly, individuals who mistakenly believe that their conscious self is merely being observed—rather than recognizing the genuine framework of their context—may see art as just a patch that enhances an already present state of mind. In reality, art often represents the initial step toward true conscious awareness. By misinterpreting its role, they inadvertently reshape their psyche to claim an inflated sense of expanded consciousness, relegating the poetic elements to a secondary status. Essentially, they adopt a superficial stance that over*shadow*s deeper, authentic awareness, thus

---

[4] Aerts, D., Broekaert, J., & Gabora, L., Intrinsic Contextuality as the Crux of Consciousness (2000). In K. Yasue (Ed.), *Fundamental Approaches to Consciousness*, (1999).

becoming their own oppressors by exhibiting undue pride and either overestimating or underestimating the extent of their actual consciousness.

A similar pattern emerges in the flow of a typical morning. As the initial burst of conscious energy fades, the contextual framework also diminishes. For those naturally attuned to consciousness, the external environment usually provides the necessary impetus for further expansion. If they instead rely on art to stimulate this process, it may interfere with the natural progression and create disruption later in the day. In such cases, employing art to trigger or repair consciousness results in a conflicting dynamic rather than supporting a smooth, natural evolution of awareness.

The Structure of Consciousness and Renunciation

The process of renunciation is paramount for the structure of consciousness. Rather than assume the sacrificial connotation, in which there is a loss that does not find its expense, in the consciousness system, it is the entire notion of renunciation that ensures alleviation for higher ground. There is an additional benefit to that element or aspect of renunciation: to be given the exchange of the entire spectrum of consciousness. Had they chosen correctly, they would have exchanged for the betterment, and thus, we would not consider it a renunciation. However, due to the lack of availability and determination of individuals or aspects, the exchange is rarely taken and more often includes what is more than they are offering. Instead, the usual outcome is the offering of consciousness substance without the exchange taking place, and thus we term it a renunciation. It is not consciousness that has made the renunciation, but only offered to retrieve the substance and allow entrance into the system.

We can see this display itself in social dynamics, for the server will have given their consciousness or vital human endeavor for the provision of the individual that is being served. The served individual is already in a structured relationship and does not have the ability to either detach or disconnect from that connection. With this in mind, we can never determine the outcome as an instance of the patron devoid of an offer of consciousness from the server, for it is already an attainment by the nature of the process of service. They could decline the service outright, but then this would not be a service dynamic per se and is not worthwhile for our inquiry. The server has the choice to either follow the expanse of consciousness, which is made available, or to retrieve from the dynamic and withhold their outlook. They cannot withhold conscious substance, for that has been made available by the service itself, but they can choose to decline engagement in the arena to which they are placed. When this occurs, we can consider the process to be a renunciation, for there is no conscious gain for the individual all the while offering their consciousness substance. We can point out the economic incentive; however, we will also notice that all economic stipends are either for metaphorical value or to offset a consciousness loss. Yet, this is a discussion for another time.

The reason that it is more likely that the server will decline the possibility of consciousness is also the reason that they retain a meager sum of consciousness. They already had many opportunities for exchange, to which they declined, finding contentment in their cosmos. This momentary exchange would be no different, for what is being offered at any occasion would make it more likely to have the individual partake in the consciousness offering; as the system is the same throughout its pivoting points. The individual who is willing to partake in the exchange in its full effect would have already reached into the realm of being required to be served, and not to serve.

Once an individual reaches a stage of expanse, they require reduced modalities of consciousness to which they will provide an embodiment of what was lost, or to be more accurate, what cannot be included in the wholeness of their conscious growth. This is provided in the manner of service and other amenities of social exchange, where they have the chance to retain the entire system of consciousness even as they remain at its peak. In this case, it is the service that has the opportunity to gain an access point to their consciousness all by engaging in that exchange.

This process is usually misunderstood, and quite easily so, by the entitlement of individuals to be those that requisite service. The need for service is only in reference to the entire expanse of consciousness, not to the status of an individual or their affluence. We see this in the concept of "new money," which represents a guise of acceptance into the realm of service not due to a consciousness expanse (for a momentary expansion of wealth does not equate to an expansion of consciousness), but rather as an amenity of service itself. In contrast, generational wealth—or "old money"—fosters a process in which individuals are subtly introduced to the dynamics of consciousness that parallel the economic market.

Over time, they learn to navigate service in a way that helps maintain a certain level of expansion. While this process cannot be explicitly taught, its parameters can be, with the hope that individuals will eventually engage in the consciousness endeavor on their own. Typically, they experience prolonged exposure to these conditions before actively participating in the consciousness process itself. Even if individuals contained by generational wealth organizations do not engage directly, their presence within the system ensures that at least one member of the family—or the broader community—will eventually interact with and contribute to the consciousness system. If not, at least an external observer may still grasp its workings through this systemic lens.

There is a very important conjecture from this: an individual of *peak consciousness*—who requires service—cannot be in a position to serve. Then, they are foregoing *peak consciousness* to a realm that cannot retrieve that information, for it is a reduced level of consciousness. This will not be considered a renunciation but rather a loss of sprawling consciousness, for immediately upon reception, it is lost due to the lack of complexity of the recipient, who is unable to integrate or process the depth of consciousness being offered. In an extreme inequitable market, in which the exchange of currency is not on par with deep contemplation of consciousness, this can be a prevailing issue. For if one is at *peak consciousness* but does not reflect in the economic market, they may enter into a serviceable exchange for the requisite economic stipend but be unavailable to retrieve that consciousness. It is rather given to those with less complexity but with certain economic fortitude. We cannot adjust the system to parallel the economic market with consciousness expansion because they follow different parameters, even if they are sourced in the same material.

PART II: RECREATED REALITY AND CONCEPTUAL MEDIATION

The Recreated Structural Reality

We can understand the stream of consciousness as follows: on one side, we have its underlying theoretical framework, which has little to do with structural reality; on the other, we have structural reality, which is foundational and actualized in a socialized realm. It is upon the stream of consciousness to recreate the structural reality so that it can converge in any possible realm because the deficiency of consciousness is that it cannot be directly linked to structural interactivity. Consciousness is a theoretical framework and therefore does not have the capacity to control, regulate, or participate in structural reality. The way in which it converges and can discuss structural reality within the individualized psyche is because consciousness recreates a structural reality within the psyche, providing a nuanced appropriation of consciousness due to individual limitations. This recreation can be done from two sides.

The First Side of Recreation: Immediate Separation

The first side of this recreation involves an immediate separation from structural reality, onto which one leaps into a conceptual realm and into the realm of consciousness that does not include or preclude any aspect of structure. Upon entering that system—by any means, whether through

The Structure of Consciousness

religious or other frameworks—granting it some credence to participate, it must recreate a structural reality to interact with individuality.

The Apollo 11 moon landing exemplifies this process. Humanity first separated from the structural reality of Earth, entering the conceptual realm of space travel, where conventional physical and societal structures no longer applied. In this new domain, although it was a psychological experience, there was a landing after all; it remained conceptual, for the structural reality of Earth remained so. The landing on the moon still represents a new version of the concept of a physical landing, such as a plane landing, only because, for our perception, we could only entertain the idea through a recreated structural lens. This is despite the actuality of the circumstance.

For instance, we could enter consciousness by noting a perfect order of nature, a systemic aspect of nature and evolution, or the character of nature. In all these cases, it is not by individual access that we entertain these notions, but simply because we entered from a single arbitrary point in the system. This means the access point is immaterial, as there was no relevance prior to that axis. There has already been a leap from structural reality, so there is no discourse to proceed with it.

Gaining Consciousness through Arbitrary Means

Upon entering, one gains a certain parameter of consciousness through arbitrary methods that may align with aspects of consciousness. As we noted in examples, these can include any universal element, with religious frameworks being a haven for such access points. Once an individual accesses consciousness without the relay of structural reality, they can begin to recreate a formulated structural reality to provide a convergence between conscious experience and structural reality. This is not the same as the memory of the structured reality from which they departed; it is a new creation based on an awareness within consciousness that requires individuality to provide a reception and thus recreate a reality for which individuality understands.

This means the recreation is based on the parameters of the wholesome conscious experience. So, in the example where nature has a character or is sequential, which is the axis point, by any means, arbitrary, one will recreate a structural reality that portrays those sequential elements alongside a certain residual memory of what structuralism consisted of.

Therefore, one might recreate the structural reality to be the concern for one another in a social sphere, but also to include the altruistic methods

The Recreated Structural Reality

known to the individual in the residual memory of structural reality. With the concern of consciousness, it is merely the sequential formula of nature that is of concern. Because we are seeking to recreate structural reality and thus provide individuality, one gains entrance through the altruistic nature of social engagement and possibility.

Altruism and Structural Service

However, this retains too much of consciousness' flavor and participation, which is not very visceral because it does not pertain to structural reality and its experience on the ground. To do this, one may retrieve from their memory base the positions pertaining to altruistic experiences so that the final recreation is a social-sequential altruism based on their experiences in that department, attached to structural reality. However, at no point is there true integration or interaction with a structured reality, only an attempt to retrieve from structured reality in order to perform a consciousness element in that department.

This means the altruism experienced prior—within the state of real structural reality—is arbitrary in nature. The experience of that only becomes a method of interest as one recreates a reality that requires those aspects alongside the more prioritized consciousness aspects. We can easily notice this when the final product of this recreation and convergence with consciousness has an individual concerned more with the sequential and balanced output of social generosity than true altruism and the necessities of individuals. It is not individuals that were ever the cause and case of interest; rather, it was consciousness that found a haven in these methods. It is the purpose of the sequence itself and the performance of that in structural reality, or at least the recreation of the structural reality, so that one has a platform for interaction with consciousness.

Departure from Consciousness and Return to Structural Reality

Once the decision is made to depart from the streamline of consciousness and its convergence with recreated reality, one becomes distinguished towards re-entering structural reality. Within structural reality, these notions are of little consequence since they never were of consequence—so why would anything change because of some revolution in consciousness? Still, in the ongoing endeavors of structural reality, one will gain some similarities between the natural manifestation of generosity on a daily basis and social reciprocation, in which those notions of consciousness reveal themselves.

For example, in the case of structural reality, a reciprocation between family bodies and generosity between familiar spaces is a natural manifestation. While one experiences those developments, they take note of the stream of consciousness and its convergence with that recreated reality, in which there is a sequential aspect and method that is profound in these endeavors. So, they may find through that simple generosity and exchange a method to perceive all of consciousness in that manner and therefore all of reality.

To illustrate the point: a family that shares meals together daily. The act of preparing and sharing food is more than an economic necessity; it reflects a deeper structural reality in which generosity flows naturally between family members. (Bohanek et al. 2009)[5].

As they engage in these shared moments, they become aware of the underlying rhythm of their mobility—a stream of consciousness that aligns with the recreated reality of familial bonds, even though that is not the intention. In this way, the simple act of giving and receiving within the home serves as a microcosm for understanding consciousness and reality as a whole.

Altruism and the Stranger: Recreated vs. Structural Reality

For this reason, we will find that all altruistic aspects that pertain to strangers—people that are not part of a familiarity system—will be naturally entertained based on one's attachment to the recreated reality within consciousness. By no means would anybody be able to engage in altruistic aspects from a structural reality standpoint. Notice that social and societal altruism is formulated out of religious frameworks or, in our case, consciousness with a convergence of a simulated reality.

Hospitals serve as a clear example of this. They were established as extensions of religious and philosophical ideals rather than as products of structural necessity, arguably the only possible form of development. The initial hospitals were often built by religious institutions, emphasizing care for the sick as a spiritual obligation rather than a mere practical response to illness, constituted by a perception of reality that wasn't from the ground up but an overlay of the land. This reflects how altruism towards strangers is

---

[5] Bohanek JG, Fivush R, Zaman W, et al. *Narrative Interaction in Family Dinnertime Conversations*, (2009).

The Recreated Structural Reality

maintained through a recreated reality—one shaped by overarching frameworks divorced from structural existence. Risse, G. B. (1999)[6]

"Because of their importance and status in a given community, hospitals have always been in the public eye... Fluctuations in image and reputation shaped admissions and generated public support... From charitable pledges and vows of religious devotion in the first millennium A.D. to humanitarian dedication since the Enlightenment, hospitals have actively portrayed themselves as houses of God and science... Hospital buildings were promoted as architectural landmarks, their monumental exteriors as expressions of religious piety and sources of civic pride... Like cathedrals, awe-inspiring interiors sought to calm the weary and the sick... At the beginning of the twentieth century, gleaming high-rise buildings and home-like interiors proclaimed a vision of asepsis, professionalism, and comfort, illustrated in brochures and annual reports... In more recent times, the media have focused almost obsessively on the drama of hospital life, particularly in emergency and operating rooms, stressing the saving of individual patients' lives, the heroics of caregivers, and the availability of state-of-the-art medical technology."

When the social reach is performed, it is not upon a structural reality but upon a recreated reality; one that could or should be. To perform altruism away from that recreation—attempting to perform in structural reality itself—will eventually cease the wholesome element and result in altruism for familiarity, as is the normal instance in structural reality. The only way that altruistic attention retains its universality is if the endeavor is fortified based on a recreated reality that does not surpass or follow the 'necessities' of individuals at a ground level. To become this—is to enter into structural reality and lose sense of consciousness.

Biological Necessities and Structural Reality

For how could structural reality and its natural experiences ascertain unfamiliar faces—ones which are not a biological benefit? The stranger and altruistic methods towards them are something that requires disorientation from structural reality and pertains to a recreated reality that associates with the streamline of consciousness. With that being the case, there is possible activation through continual interactions with generosity at a structural

---

[6] Risse, G. B. (1999). Mending bodies, saving souls: A history of hospitals. Oxford University Press.

level, where these notions of consciousness permeate at a natural instinct so that a sequential formula of consciousness gains entry.

At some point, those two lines—that of recreated reality and that of structural reality—will parallel in enough similarity that it will become almost instinctual to ascertain an altruistic system that does not pertain to individuality but rather to a sequential persona of nature: *to be nice*. However, because the biological limits remain, it will never be the case that there is a biological necessity for altruistic methods at such an extensive scale. The convergence will never be enacted at the full extent.

Seeking Convergence between Structural and Recreated Reality

Dissatisfaction with this partial convergence may drive some to attempt to impose a merger between the two realities. They strive to overlay the recreated reality onto structural reality—essentially ignoring the inherent qualities of the latter and performing as if it were already recreated within consciousness. In doing so, these individuals begin to reconstruct structural reality not as it is, but as a performance meant to connect with consciousness. When the disparity and impossibility of complete convergence become recognized, instead of departing from consciousness to fully embrace structurality, one might choose to dismiss that reality altogether. This leads to an even more pronounced development of the recreation process, albeit one that does not remain firmly anchored to the processes on the ground.

For example, consider the hospital at the other extreme—a place so entrenched in its structural reality that it becomes, for the individual, akin to a foreign land. This overindulgence in recreation, as opposed to the acceptance of its structural origins, transforms the experience. As Guenter B. Risse describes, "going to a hospital resembles a journey to a foreign, exotic land, an all-too-common pilgrimage in which patients cross into a world of strange rites, miraculous interventions, and frequent death. For those who tell or write their stories, this approach allows them to attach a social value to the events surrounding their hospitalization, making the experiences transitory and capable of being endured with courage and patience. From admission to discharge, the unknown and often hostile environment must be navigated from a position of weakness and disadvantage. The conception of the hospital as a house of crises and rituals is therefore useful not only for interpreting the choreography of institutional routines but also for understanding the experience of hospitalization for patients" (Risse, 1999, p. 9–10).

Over time, as the recreation process loosens its ties to structural reality, it becomes solely an expression of consciousness attempting to recreate reality. In this state, one may find themselves in opposition to structural reality—denying its influence and using alternate methods to continue the process of recreation without regularly recalibrating against the ground reality.

This is one manner in which the process of consciousness is engaged: the reins of recreation no longer align with structural reality. Alternatively, an individual might achieve such a vast level of awareness that, when attempting to recreate structural reality, they overlook essential details. This negligence results in a recreated version that fails to match the depth of the conscious expansion they are pursuing. Consequently, it is not merely the disparity between structural and recreated reality that defines the outcome, but an overwhelming surge of consciousness that over*shadow*s a performative, accurate recreation of structural reality.

The Outcome: Consciousness Overlays Structural Reality

The outcome is as follows: The recreation of a reality loses its substantiation in the process, and instead, the consciousness endeavor begins to overlay upon structural reality itself or one's anchor upon structurality. That is to say, one will retrieve from their understanding of structural reality to provide a haven for consciousness, meaning it will be a direct interaction between consciousness and reality itself. This would have an individual converge between consciousness and structural reality so that one's very attachments—whether perceptual or otherwise—will include conscious sentiments, despite the fact that structurality does not have the bandwidth to include or ascertain towards consciousness itself because it requires individuality with its complex social situation.

In our example, the case would be as follows: one gains entrance into consciousness and understands very complex aspects of nature and its sequential aspects in how they perform in each other and so forth, e.g., physics. Yet, they will have as their recreation of reality, a simplistic version of altruism, where kindness assists the world in some manner. Because the understanding at the conscious level is far greater than the

The Structure of Consciousness

recreated reality it is attempting to converge upon, those sequential markers and coinciding understanding will converge upon structural reality.

These mediators of sequential understandings are a great regard and are up-performing in social dynamics and their sphere, even as they have no ability to retain and ascertain those elements. The manifestation will be such that the individual performs their experiences with reality itself—at least structural reality—in a manner that includes all that consciousness substance, forcing themselves upon reality to restructure it to perform as consciousness would. Fairly similar to the other case, in which one ascertains a recreated structural reality because they find deficiency in the convergence between that and reality, but in this case, reality itself becomes the parameter upon which consciousness substance is placed, at its expense.

There are two manners in which to ensure that consciousness substance does not permeate structural reality: one is an enforcement of a recreated reality so that the convergence maintains itself at the baseline of a simulation and goes no further, and secondly, at the structural level, in which there is maintenance that disallows permission of consciousness material.

To disallow engagement with conscious material and thus ascertain structural reality is to engage in the systemic process without any integral aspects that perceive it, but rather as the substance itself. Instead of any overlord perception of the engagements, structural reality will make itself known prior to any conceptual basis.

If one is contextually inclined, then their engagement with structural reality will be apportioned based on a context that stems from a consciousness substance at some point or another. This would mean that their entire engagement with structural reality is based on a stretched consciousness endeavor instead of a direct engagement with structural reality. If one were to interact with the context of work and mind, it would also be a stretch from a prior consciousness point of conjecture, disillusioning oneself from structural reality. In fact, if we follow this assumption, we will notice that far fewer individuals are able to engage with structural reality in a proper forum.

The interactions that seep through a context will not be aspects of structural reality but rather will be based on the continuation of that consciousness endeavor. Indeed, we must find structural reality in the basic biological necessities to which an outstretched context always meets that premise. When a context is relatively new in its proposal and its connection to an interactive experience, it will not necessarily conform to biological

The Recreated Structural Reality

parameters. However, when the context reaches the end, it begins to approach biological necessities, for that is where it will gain further vitality.

This is why we notice that fields of work, which require little contextual stimulation or interactive backgrounds, will be infused with biological sentiments—work of the hands, focus of the body, necessities of the body, and so forth. Even the language spoken will pertain to biological aspects because there is a weakening contextual layer to the entire premise of that workflow.

In fact, we can consider fields of work that have a limited contextual overlay as further removed from the philosophical premise of work and closer to simple biological actions. These actions pertain to a parameter set by a field of work but are, in essence, a constitution of personal biological happenstance.

This is why there is a societal call for such work to be considered "real work," almost in an ironic undertone, in which it is furthest from the philosophical notion of work but closest to the biological experience, which has nothing to do with work parameters. We term "real work" because it requires an aptitude and fortitude to maintain a continual workflow, despite the fact that it does not provide the parameters of a philosophical notion of work. It is real, rather than work, and there is a certain oxymoron to proclaiming "real work."

As we noticed, it is not necessarily the case that simple familiarity structures would be constituted as structural reality, because we have the notion of "real work" as another premise. It is not bound to familiarity parameters but still constitutes structural reality because of its biological makeup. Of course, there is a quest for familiarity in these environments because they are biologically shaped, and individuals will not find it favorable to engage in a stranger's experience while they indulge in biological developments.

In fact, we can consider any environment as structural reality when the notion of being a stranger becomes problematic to its structure. It will continuously seek to familiarize what is strange and disassociate from what cannot be familiarized. The quest for familiarity is a biological experience, and there is no way to reciprocate if it pertains to a stranger's development. That is a matter of consciousness, not structural reality.

Those focused on structurality will prioritize the entire environmental and social realm toward what they can constitute as non-strangers. Even as hundreds of individuals pass by, they will be on the lookout for what constitutes familiarity, thus making it available for structural reality and

The Structure of Consciousness

biological experience. This is especially true for those who partake in biological reciprocation with society in the "real work" we noted earlier.

We will observe these three layers in any grouping within society where structural reality is present. These are the elements of reciprocation in a biological manner, with individuals constituting each other as familiarity, making them available for reciprocation in that way. There are also the biological necessities for all individuals in that environment—whether it is freedom of movement, lack of freedom, positioning (standing or sitting), access to airflow, food supply, or any other biological aspects. All individuals are subject to this premise, and therefore, all engage with structural reality despite the presence of other layers.

The second layer, an intermediary, is the recreation of structural reality. This is the constitution that an individual proclaims upon that environment. It is not necessarily the truth of the matter, nor does it need to align perfectly, but rather it forms a perception of reality that does not balance itself with structural premises. This includes an understanding of what a city is, or what a society is, or what a group consists of—these are premises that are not necessarily grounded in structural reality, but are enough to align with structurality while still departing as a recreation.

Either these recreations tend to be general, losing their credibility as a representation, or they are fairly similar, appearing as another form of structural reality.

For instance, if an individual perceives the surrounding society as the constituents of a city, grouped under a singular premise, it is true that this is a recreation of structural reality. However, it misaligns from parallel themes. Structural reality is based on biological reciprocations, so recreating the city as a structure requires an adherence to those biological aspects. This is why police and fire departments are often considered central when recreating a city's structure. They are biologically aligned, reciprocating according to fundamental necessities that permeate throughout the system, making it easy to constitute the entire city based on those aspects.

Other notions that help reconstruct the idea of a city include monuments or architectural feats. These are biologically imprinted, providing biological amenities while also serving something more—they offer an entrance into consciousness. This is why we cannot imagine a city without monuments or architectural feats. They are prime elements that offer both biological

The Recreated Structural Reality

and structural reality, as well as entertainment for the recreation of that structural reality and an affordance to consciousness.

One can perceive the same building in either layer: as a biological event in a structural reality or as a consciousness addendum providing the recreation of reality for the consciousness sentiment. We can even perceive the two primary groups in any city or society—strangers and regular members. Strangers are those who visit and most easily notice the recreation of reality because they see what stands out the most. They generalize a system, which is the natural manifestation of a new experience for nuances not yet available.

On the other hand, regular members of a society or group focus more on structural reality and biological reciprocation. They begin to see occurrences as simply extensions of the family body and mediocre biological experiences.

Without the recreation of structural reality, there would be no convergence with consciousness, as consciousness does not directly align with structural reality. We can take the monumental structure as an example: its biological reciprocation cannot align with consciousness because they are fundamentally of different proportions. Instead, the mediator is the recreation of that structural reality, which requires architectural imagination that stretches beyond those limitations, thus becoming a haven for consciousness sentiment. The convergence occurs within the structure, where the structural reality and the convergence of consciousness to the recreated reality parallel in a way that feeds each other.

Architectural Feats and Functional Limitations

This is why architectural feats that stray from functionality do not activate into what we are defining 'structural reality'. Even though they align structurally, they do not align proportionally, as there is no need to move from function to dysfunction in that container of consciousness. For instance, postmodern architecture often had a limited lifespan, with some buildings constructed as ephemeral structures intended to last only about 25 years. This is a case of being untethered to structural reality, for it only serves a dialogical form that is highly volatile for those who participate and are interested in a conceptual form of insight. (Szacka, 2019)[7]

An example that proves otherwise is Gothic architecture, which has a profound effect on reality because it serves as a marker of the absence of

---

[7] Szacka L-C. *Insight: Life, Earth, and Ephemerality of Postmodern Architecture.* (2018)

The Structure of Consciousness

history upon which Western developments rely. On the other hand, architectural features that are purely functional cannot be considered architectural feats because they do not recreate structurality. They merely perfect basic biological experiences and, therefore, do not engage with the notion of recreating reality. This means they are not available for convergence with consciousness.

We cannot even engage in an analysis of the necessities of structural reality without recreating it in a way that is available for convergence with consciousness. If we attempt to follow structural reality as it presents itself, we enter into the biological necessities that pertain to individual bases. We can gather biological experiences and reciprocation, as well as familiar spaces, but the very act of gathering that material would require the recreation of that reality. The most we can achieve is participation in structural reality itself, allowing us to gain personal existential awareness of a portion of that biological state. However, this does not encompass all biological experiences or the entirety of structural reality. As long as there is true participation, we gain knowledge of that structural reality that can be used for purposeful recreation.

For example, we can perceive the monumental structure as a biological experience with a purposeful objective within structural reality, but it will only serve as a case in point, not representing the entirety of that structural reality. It is true that as long as we entertain the experience without convergence with consciousness, we are only encapsulating a portion of that structural reality. It can never encompass the entire reality. Therefore, futile attempts to understand the monument based on biological experience will not be fulfilling or stimulating to consciousness. The understanding we assume to have gained is not available for deliberation because it is solely the basis of structural reality that cannot see more than itself.

The only way we can proclaim an understanding of that monument is if we depart from the biological experiences and structural reality to recreate that reality and its monumental aspects, making them available for convergence with consciousness. We use biological experiences to formalize this recreation, but with the awareness that it is merely a stimulatory aspect of a larger whole.

Consciousness, Context, and the Perceptual Psyche

There are two types of downgraded interactivity from a conscious sequence: one that is chosen, for instance, during the night or on weekends, and the other that is imposed by the environment, such as extreme weather patterns or social upheaval.

Thus, perceptual and internal realms each constrain the other. Perceptual interactivity might permit internal processing, but not alignment. One form of mediation involves parallel interaction: perception is received, then internal context is applied. But this delays internal autonomy, leaving it reactive and dependent on perceptual input. The psyche becomes governed by perception, which manipulates internal states and social interactions alike.

Perceptual interactivity is volatile. Real-time engagement is difficult. If context chases during every perceptual stimulus, it becomes reactive. A better approach allows context to precede perception—to anticipate and regulate perceptual input. *Contextual mediation* identifies points of contention and reframes them without nullifying their meaning.

Thus, the first step in mediating volatile perceptual interactivity is separation. Constructing development directly atop exposed interactivity risks amplifying its volatility. Trauma exemplifies this and revisiting traumatic exposure often magnifies it. Instead, the psyche must continue its internal sequencing despite trauma's presence—or treat trauma—not through it. Mediation demands internal separation while continuing development, reaffirming a general rule: do not cultivate traumatic exposure. Move onward, finding mediation within the psyche's architecture.

However, when one accepts—or more accurately, ignores—perceptual interactivity, they do so at the expense of the bond between the psyche and the perceptual arena. The perceptual arena's concern is with providing the psyche with data about reality and its interactivity, but this is dutifully declined for a so forth reason. The deference of information becomes the cause of antagonism between the internal arena and perception in general. This results in a detachment from reality altogether, and the psyche begins to adhere to its internality as if it was the only reality.

Thus, we have two realms that serve each other—each not allowing the other full scope of interactivity. Perceptual interactivity allows for internal interactivity that as a minimum does not align with its information. For this reason, there is a potential mediation between the two, achieved by aligning internal interactivity parallel to perceptual interactivity.

However, if one simply ingests perceptual interactivity and applies their internal continuance based on an established context, it does not alleviate the genuine internal workings of the psyche. This process only attempts to bridge the gap by absorbing the information and then applying internal adjustments subsequently. The psyche operates at a constant pace by engineering context and interactivity that parallels the experience. Ultimately, the result is a prolonged perceptual interactivity, for at no point did the context and internal interactivity stand alone, as they adhered to the perceptual interactivity for direction.

Now, for the process of enlarging and developing perceptual interactivity, this would be a steadfast process—but it would not serve as mediation between internality and perceptual interactivity. Instead, the outcome, if prolonged, would result in the expansion of perceptual interactivity, where that realm begins to regulate and control the individual—especially when all the perception mechanism notices how germane all of their ordinary interactions become from unassuming exchanges.

In addition to the inevitable manipulation of surrounding sociality, one will also manipulate perceptual experiences in order to gain some device over their internal state. The point of contention is the perceptual realm, where both the individual and sociality will attempt to gain control over the internal system. At no point is there a genuine formation of an internal system that is independent of perceptual interactivity.

Now, the psyche and the perceptual realm share a very strong dynamic—so much so that we can be certain that all information is altered in accordance with the entire system. Secondly, perceptual interactivity has not considered the full scope of the internal psyche and its interactions, which—when fully developed—has reached trillions of points. In this way, one is attempting to enter a system that contains and retains trillions of conjectures. To suggest that the trillion-point internal system is somehow the landscape of current perceptual interactivity is disconcerting, and would require a metaphysical argument to even attempt its logicality.

The outcome of deferring to momentary and sometimes arbitrary perceptual interactivity in the interface of the psyche system is a loss of the internal system, which then becomes more reliant on perceptual information for continued interactivity. Although it is true that the psyche system is composed of masses of junctures of interactivity that were once perceptual material, it cannot be said that any conjecture of perceptual interactivity should be deferred to that system. Furthermore, this neglects the internal development that has been underway the entire time, where the perceptual information that gained entrance is not the same as what is currently propagating within the psyche.

Because perceptual interactivity is going to be most volatile and disruptive at the interactive point, this may not be the most productive for mediation. Meaning to say that at any time and place, there is going to be a natural interactive point that is most salient in interactivity and demanding of experience for the psyche's happenstance.

If one were to attempt to apply a *contextual mediation* to perceptual information flow that is afforded to interactivity that is most directive, what happens is one will begin to follow the procedure of conjectures of perceptual interactivity to a point where they will find it hard to provide *contextual mediation*—as well as misdirection by the control of interactivity. The second point is more important, for when the perceptual realm gains control of the contexts, then it is no longer a *contextual mediation* but rather an exposure that is immediately contextualized. And if we follow the nanoseconds of the scientific mind, we would find that the reception arrived first and the context was layered upon it to regulate.

Choosing Context: Navigating Forced and Voluntary Interactivity

When interactivity is forced—such as by a change in weather patterns—it does not emerge from the realm of consciousness but instead acts as a pressure against it. The difference between choice and non-choice lies in the contextual understanding of a situation. Recognizing one's decision to participate in interactivity, despite the prevalence of conscious awareness, is what distinguishes a chosen experience from an imposed boundary.

Chosen interactivity, such as that which takes place at night, enters a realm where it is agreed that communication with consciousness is occurring.

Yet this communication still exists within a specific framework of consciousness. Because the *shadow*-realm's offerings are layered by means of individual consciousness and grounded in *shadow*-based phenomena, one cannot remain static within it; they will be carried along except while connected to the material environment of consciousness, maintaining a context rooted in that realm—even amid environmental dissonance.

Courage is essential. Without resisting forced interactivity, one cannot transcend such to sustain a context that reconnects with genuine consciousness. Those who adopt forced interactivity—particularly during extreme conditions like war, pandemics, or environmental upheaval—will struggle to return to a context aligned with consciousness beyond individual experience. Such interactivity typically does not belong to the realm of shared consciousness, but instead leads people into personal engagements unless they consciously redirect back toward a collective conscious framework.

Non-choiced interactivity challenges the boundaries of consciousness and draws its energy from a realm distinct from it. For example, a dramatic weather event can limit consciousness by triggering primal emotions—fear, awe, dread—emotions that do not inherently belong to the original conscious domain.

Choice, then, becomes the mechanism by which one either returns to the prevailing consciousness (as might occur at night or on weekends) or transitions into an independently anchored consciousness. We cannot claim that the environment as a whole shifts into an alternate realm, for each entity's interaction is grounded in their own awareness—even in response to war or natural upheaval. The environment may act according to its internal value system, but individuals are not compelled to follow. Instead, they may choose contexts that reaffirm the shared realm and resist the gravitational pull toward a fragmented, personalized consciousness.

When the environment "chooses"—or is compelled—to initiate interactivity that deviates from the current consciousness, it becomes a *shadow realm*. Here, interactivity is forced, determined not by collective awareness but by individual consciousness, remaining only a *shadow* of the conscious realm. True expansion in such that an environment must still accelerate from genuine consciousness, not its reflection.

This prompts a question: can an individual generate a context that leads back to shared consciousness, even when the dominant realm has become a *shadow*—one enforcing interactivity based on isolated consciousness rather than the collective? Even as the environment aligns itself against consciousness through alternate forms of interactivity, it remains possible for individuals to assert independent contexts.

Yet a caveat persists: if the *shadow realm* enforces interactivity grounded in the individual, any context formed within it tends to reinforce that very *shadow realm*. Nonetheless, consciousness expands inherently—contexts always move toward an entity's conscious domain, not away from it. But when one internalizes the *shadow realm*'s dynamics, their context ceases to be a sanctuary; it becomes a trap—a gateway into the *shadow realm*.

Only by detaching the expansion of consciousness from that system does true contextual agency emerge. The *shadow realm* offers no solution through context alone. Only existential or physical separation can weaken its influence. But even existential withdrawal often fails, for mere presence in the realm can reactivate its consciousness—by that point, the psyche is already affected. Actualized consciousness, once embedded, becomes part of the internal psyche and circulates within.

Only when an individual carries a context born from the conscious realm can they voluntarily engage in a forced experience. But deepening that engagement risks entanglement—disconnecting one from the very consciousness that granted them the context in the first place.

Navigating Internal Autonomy and Perceptual Exposure

At any point on the continuum of psyche experience, one must choose between two kinds of interactivity: one that manifests outwardly, and one governed by an internal contextual overlay. These often conflict: raw external interactivity can suppress what the internal psyche is trying to process.

The inverse is also true. In the absence of perceptual intrusion, the psyche can fully explore interaction. This creates a state unbound by perceptual constraints, where internal interactions stretch as far as imagination allows. Without needing to mediate between internal and external domains, internal engagement can flourish. Yet this freedom risks overextending a contextual perspective that may not be robust enough to handle full domestication.

For instance, consider a theory of nature that presents it as a singular cosmic system, reducing individuality to a minor role. While theoretically sound, this can result in interactions where individuality is undermined. Although the theory itself may not aim to dominate social development, excessive interactivity can blur the distinctions necessary for higher-level social life—a disturbing outcome for many.

Still, contexts can be organized well enough to prevent drastic consequences, even at high levels of interaction. For example, a broad theory of sexuality that enhances and validates social experience might regulate itself. Even when heavily domesticated, its complexity could provoke social dynamics that act as a check on its extremes—preserving overall function. In such cases, even extreme domestication has minimal repercussions.

From this, two conclusions emerge: [1] either the context is not perfectly structured, [2] or internal interactivity is hindered by residual perceptual interference.

Perceptual interaction, on the other hand, can become overstimulating. One may follow this hyperactive context into a confining state, or retreat entirely into privatized internality—severing their bond with the external world. Since perception provides crucial data, ignoring such causes tension between inner and outer realms, leading the psyche to treat its internal state as the ultimate reality.

The relationship between psyche and perception is asymmetrical but powerful. Perception alters internal content, while internal context filters or rejects perceptual complexity. To suggest that countless internal processes are shaped by brief perceptual inputs is questionable—internal reflections endure, altered only subtly over time.

Some claim the psyche passively processes perception. But this overlooks the variety of perceptual material. A deeply embedded translator may only reinforce existing structures, reducing perception to a servant of the internal world. Incoming data either confirms the internal model or is dismissed—common in highly contextualized individuals with fixed aims.

Still, this has merit. It limits internal freedom to filter information for relevance. But genuine mediation must focus on internal organization—not perceptual suppression.

To mediate from within, one must choose: either controlled perception or autonomy. Controlling perception imposes internal context too premature; while allowing full autonomy risks overwhelming the system. A middle path—*contextual mediation*—is preferable: a contextual overlay that moderates perception without disrupting it. It reframes experience without hijacking it, akin to a doorway.

Consider a hostile interaction between two people—perception becomes entangled in the conflict. A contextual mediator might redirect attention to something unrelated, such as fashion. Initially trivial, fashion is subtly informative and interactive. This reframing maintains engagement while reducing volatility. If context justifies the shift, the benefit outweighs the cost of ignoring hostility.

However, the context must be consciously chosen. Arbitrary overlays misalign with psyche development and become counterproductive. If the context arises unconsciously or reactively, it becomes another form of perceptual domination.

A well-organized context can prevent drastic consequences even in the height of interactivity. Take again the example of sexuality: in extreme cases, social dynamics may resist its over-domestication. The libido may be curbed to allow more adaptable structures. Thus, even comprehensive theories may contain built-in safeguards. Still, if consequences arise, it may be due to flawed contextual design or residual perceptual interference limiting internal freedom.

Similarly, overstimulated perceptual interaction may either lead to confinement or drive someone to privatized internal interactivity, where perceptual data is ignored and development continues as if untouched by external stimuli. Highly contextualized individuals often interpret perceptual data either as confirmation of their system or as an obstacle to their goals.

This is not a failure to recognize interactivity's autonomy, but rather a regulation of internality—only a limited flow of perceptual data is allowed. Yet, as previously argued, mediation is still possible. The internal realm operates independently, receiving but only through translation. The solution must lie in internal structuring.

Thus, the psyche's relationship with perception is central to mediation. A contextual oversight is needed—not disruptive stimulation, but one that preserves genuine interactive experience. This is what we call *contextual mediation*: a moderating overlay that aligns with perception's flow without interfering in its direct relationship with the system. Without such direct interaction, we do not truly access perception, but only parallel it—a kind of internal mimicry that does not serve the real system.

What we seek, then, is a context that precedes perception—an oversight that regulates exposure in real-time. This interactivity must arise from general experience, not from perceptual conjecture.

In *contextual mediation*, context is not summoned after perception but *before* it—acting as a lens to assess what perception offers. It identifies interactive elements that align with the internal framework and disregards volatile, non-expansive inputs. But this does not mean eliminating exposure. Direct interaction between external input and the psyche must remain intact.

Returning to our previous example: if hostility erupts between two people, and one immediately interprets it through a personal context, the psyche receives a full gust of hostility—without mediation. The goal is not increased attachment to perception, but a working mediation between perception and psyche.

To achieve this, one must suppress the impulse to react to hostility, justify detachment, and instead seek interaction aligned with a chosen context—such as observing 'fashion'. This allows for perceptual engagement that avoids triggering volatile conjecture.

'Fashion', a subtle yet active interactive cue, provides mediation without overwhelming the psyche. In contrast, choosing a topic like insect study in the midst of a hostile environment would yield little mediation—it's too far removed from real-time perceptual cues. Thus, personal and societal development depends on interactive elements appropriate to the moment and place.

Even humorously, one could navigate a hostile moment by focusing on the others' wardrobe, finding interaction through style rather than conflict. This demands resilience, as the psyche must not be overexposed to antagonism. That exposure must remain limited, justified only by the chosen context. The choice, then, is to dismiss hostility and pursue other interactions—staying seated within experience while focused on alternate

Consciousness, Context, and the Perceptual Psyche

contextual cues. In doing so, perceptual engagement occurs without deferring to the internal world or subordinating perception to internal aims. Mediation becomes possible.

Of course, exposure always comes at a cost. Without it, mediation fails. But that cost must be justified by the context from which it emerged. If that context is arbitrary or unconsciously motivated, then exposure becomes problematic for development—a discussion for another time.

Ultimately, any psyche development built upon an already exposed context can be developed with such organization that, even at a high pace of interactivity, it would not reach a consequence that could prove drastic. For example, consider the general theory of sexuality, where its enlargement and validation are distinctive developments for sociality. It is possible that domesticating or interacting could conjure a form of sexuality that follows that nuance to such an extent that sociality would not be able to endure its dynamic exchange. When this happens, it is only constrained by the dynamic exchange and prevented from resulting in any consequence beyond that.

The process would involve sexuality at an extreme, (with possible law-breaking) which, finding itself unable to function within its dynamics, would ultimately lead to the decision to curb the libido in order to allow for more dynamic structures. It gives the impression that even with all conceivable domestication of such a theory, it retains safeguards that have no significant consequences. (For the psyche, not society, e.g., sexual assault retains a dynamic) Therefore, it can be argued that the context itself may be questioned for its perfect organization, or such that internal interactivity is not given free rein due to perceptual interference.

The same can be said for perceptual interaction that is overstimulated, where an individual can follow such interactivity and its context to a conjecture that fulfills a sensibility of interactivity, thus enlarging that confinement. Alternatively, the individual can follow an internal interactivity based on a context that is preserved for their privatization, allowing them to continue the process of development as if there is no stimulating perceptual material.

In this way, the internal realm is functioning accordingly but without genuine engagement with perceptual information. This process is common among highly contextualized individuals who have a strong focus upon objectives, where despite the perceptual data at face value, it is directly

The Structure of Consciousness

interpreted as either a continuing validation of their system or a conflict that disrupts their objectives.

There is merit to this approach because they are not failing to account for the autonomy of interactivity and its internal consequences, but instead have regulated the internal realm so that only a limited amount of information is allowed to be exposed; all relevant to the contextual mainstay. However, we previously suggested that mediation is possible, alleviating many of these consequences. Since the internal realm functions as a system on its own, which receives, but only through translation, and is afforded autonomy in its operations, the solution must focus on internal arrangement.

The relationship to the perceptual realm, thus, is paramount to this mediation and would require a certain contextual oversight—while not with stimulation that would disrupt the genuine interactive experience that flows from externality. This, we would call *contextual mediation*, where according to the perceptual flow of information, a contextual overlay provides mediation but not disruption of its direct interaction with the system itself. If there is no sustained, uninterrupted interaction, the process becomes futile—mistakenly presenting itself as a reception of external reality, when in fact it is a form of psyche manipulation that merely parallels perceptual information without engaging directly or functionally.

What we are seeking now is a context that originates foremost, in which the reception is exposed to a certain degree but regulated in real-time. For this to occur, the interactivity cannot be the conjectures of the perceptual realm, but rather an interactive point that could arise simply from a general interactive experience.

The purpose of the process of mediation is that interactivity is not the first instance in which context must be conjured in accordance—but rather, context is the approach to the perceptual realm, almost as an oversight lurking below, to see what aspects can be retrieved. Thus, it finds interactive experiences in the perceptual realm that mediate by means of that context. That context cannot be regulated to a point where it takes interactive aspects that are non-interactive—meaning they have no bearing on the expansion of current experience—as well, if they are not allowed a certain exposure that is direct from the interaction to psyche parts.

For example, if one were to be in an environment where two individuals become hostile for whatever reason, the interactivity of that experience at its most conjectured point is going to be that hostile interaction. However, if one were to immediately receive the exposure of that hostile interactivity

Consciousness, Context, and the Perceptual Psyche

and apply a context that gives it justification, an understanding for transferring a reception to the psyche, the finale of that experience is limited exposure of hostility.

We are not looking to become more attached to the perceptual realm, but rather to create a mediation between the two. For this to happen, the hostile conjecture needs to be sidelined, as difficult as that may be—ignored for its haphazard nature—whatever reason to justify detaching from that interactivity—and then utilizing the demand of interactivity for a contextual oversight of specific points that are irrespective of that highly volatile interactive point.

Hence, in this environment—to complete the example—they may find themselves with a context to understand the revolution of fashion of that era, in which they attempt to study the environment and survey its interactivity for fashionable aspects, until they arrive at a contextual orientation that effectively mediates through the interactivity, ultimately yielding both informational development and subtle instances of interactivity rooted in that fashionable aspect. Notice that we've mentioned fashionable aspects because they are something that is usually interactive within an environment, even though it is subtle in nature. It would be quite problematic for the context to approach the study of insects in that environment, for if they partake a context of that sort and try to gain interactivity from it, it will not mediate perceptual activity but rather an internal structure that depends on external formation for its content—without ever being truly exposed to the interactivity itself. This is why the development of any individual or society is reliant and dependent on the interactive aspects of being—so that there is a certain method that will be followed despite the era.

In a somewhat humorous way, one might address the hostility by shifting focus to observing their wardrobe, thereby engaging with the interactivity of fashion instead. However, this is going to require a stronger mediation and resilience in the interactivity, so that at no point does the hostility itself become a conjecture of exposure—for the exposed elements will become such without the choice of the individual.

The choice of the individual is, in the immediate notice of that hostility, to arbitrarily dismiss it—whatever their justification is for detaching from that interactivity—but still remain at the seat of experience with their context to focus on interactive elements that are related.

In this manner, there is a gain of interactivity from the perceptual realm that does not defer to the internal realm, nor does it become secondary in relation to the internal realm—and thus, the mediation is possible. Of course, there is a certain cost to the exposed elements, for if there's no exposure then we have not approached the subject properly. That cost is justified for the context in which that expense came.

Now, the discussion of why one found this specific context is also important—because if it was arbitrarily motivated or motivated from non-conscious realms of psyche, then the exposure and the experience become problematic for the sequential development of the individual. However, this is a conversation for another time and work.

Any development of psyche material in congruence with an already exposed element of interactivity—even if it is presumed to be a context on its own—will still be foundationally offset from the exposed aspect. Therefore, any development of psyche material based on conjectured interactivity is always going to be problematic from the outset. By simply developing upon that—without the realization, or even with the realization of the exposure—it becomes the case where the interactivity of exposure is enlarged and not in service to the internality of the psyche and its happenstance.

Perceptual vs. Internal Interaction

This tension explains why certain experiences evoke dread—especially those that demand engagement with narrowly defined interactions. Any form of bondage—whether imposed by social structures, natural forces, or the extraterrestrials of the body or psyche—is dreadful precisely because it restricts the scope of individual interaction. Such bondage organizes the psyche into specific patterns, constrained by their constructed nature.

The experience of bondage is a direct interaction with entities that have engineered or imposed that confinement. Their overwhelming imprint on the perceptual field can seem to preclude any other substance of interaction. Perception becomes preoccupied with a single circumstance, demanding the suppression of all other possibilities and presenting the current environment as the only interactive reality.

Some argue that internal interactivity must remain tied to external experience. Yet the psyche suggests otherwise: it operates on its own frequency, interpreting perceptual input through translation. Like a translator adjusting language for the listener, the psyche reshapes

Consciousness, Context, and the Perceptual Psyche

perceptual content to fit its internal framework. A strong translator–receiver dynamic personalizes the message—but at the cost of distortion.

Some may argue that all internal interactivity is solely based on external experience and thus should not be severed from its dependency. Nevertheless, the truth of the psyche's construction is that its internal system does not operate at the wavelength of perceptual information. Instead, it is designed to be detached from external experience. The only manner in which it receives perceptual information is through a method of reception, where that material is interpreted and translated according to the internal system at large.

Analogous to the role of a translator—where the process of translation is contingent upon the relational dynamic between the translator and the recipient—the content is rendered with deliberate consideration. Nevertheless, the final articulation of the translated material inevitably conforms to the parameters of that relational dynamic. It is not uncommon to observe subtle or even substantial modifications in the translated content as a result. Consequently, when evaluating the reception of translated material, it cannot be asserted that the information has been preserved in its original form; rather, it has been shaped in accordance with the recipient's interpretive framework.

In instances where the dynamic between the translator and the recipient is particularly strong, it can be reasonably inferred that the entirety of the individual's personhood has been taken into account prior to the articulation of the information. Accordingly, the greater the strength of this dynamic, the higher the likelihood that the original content has been significantly altered in order to render it most compatible with the recipient's cognitive and emotional framework.

We could argue that the psyche has an internality that has developed accordingly so that when perceptual information enters, it is automatically translated into the internal formation, without the need for mediation. This argument does not delve into the complexity and diversity of perceptual information, for the reason that we cannot simply translate all perceptual information to a specific focus point that has already been developed.

In the case of the translator, if they were so deeply embedded in the persona of the one receiving the material, they would not provide a coherent translation, but rather a continuing validation for what the individual at present wants to receive. It would be as if the translation process itself were arbitrary. The perceptual domain becomes a servant of the internal domain,

The Structure of Consciousness

in which, despite the content, becomes a reception that aligns with the intended reception.

After we have covered that, let us proceed to a possible solution of mediation. As we've noted, if there's going to be mediation, it must be from the internal organization rather than anything perceptually related. Even in the case we just mentioned, it was only because of individuals who were willing to follow a certain, fairly elementary degree of internality that anything was made possible. No—if we are going to construct mediation from the internal realm, it must not meet the disruption of the perceptual process. Either we can disrupt the perceptual process by dictating the terms at which to perceive, or allow perception complete autonomy so that the influence of externality completely overwhelms the psyche parts, as in the case of trauma.

With all this noted, there is still the reality of perceptual conjecture that requires a certain mediation. Firstly, because the exposure is demanding at the doorway of the psyche, so that if one lets loose for a moment of their mediation, they end up with that exposure as well. There is a reason that these elements are the point of conjecture, and for that alone they need to be dealt with.

However, the dealing shall not be in the case of that exposure itself, but instead, separate from it at the time of the dealings, such that the interactivity is not alive in real-time. This would mean that one would need to detach from the exposure of that interactive conjecture so that they find themselves at the base psyche experience and not following the already exposed material which demands a direction in that interactivity.

This is why one cannot develop trauma in whatever regard, for if it was already an exposed material for the psyche, any approach at those elemental aspects with more development will only enlarge the exposure and will not provide a development of the eternal psyche that is irrespective of the trauma and would like to continue despite its intrusion.

This is a very difficult thing to bear, for by the mere fact of exposure, it gives one the inability to proceed and develop away from the exposed elements. Rather, one must sideline it and continue psyche sequences despite its prevalence.

The other possibility is for one to detach from any interactivity or sentimental value that is given to that psyche intrusion, so that the development is irrespective of the psyche part. However, because trauma is a high level of exposure, it becomes an automatic catalyst when one simply attempts to engage at a detached level in which the engagement is forthcoming.

Therefore, a very strong degree of separation is needed, in which it becomes as if arbitrary that the trauma is there—and the exposure is rather but a nothingness and void of the psyche—so that when one attempts to develop themes that are related to the development of that exposure, it is not paralleled or in function with that psyche part.

This is why it's a generally good rule to note that one does not have the accessibility to gain entrance and develop traumatic exposure, but rather to continue unabated despite its prevalence and disruptions. However, the exposure will not disintegrate nor go away unless it is mediated between psyche parts.

Social Buffers & Higher-Order Mediation

One possible path forward involves constructing a social buffer that filters perceptual input and supports internal development. Sociality ought to offer dynamic exchanges that facilitate both perceptual engagement and internal organization. This dynamic exchange—foundational to civilization and higher consciousness—is rare. Most social systems prioritize comfort over growth, resulting in stagnant reciprocity and limited internal evolution. Such groups rarely leave a historical trace except as anthropological footnotes.

Before we continue, we have to consider the form of sociality in which one surrounds themselves in a buffer of society that would dictate their perceptual information and thus allow for mediation. There is a matter in which to construct that sociality such that it affords itself to be an agreement to dynamic functionality—so that each proponent is offering interactivity to the perceptual realm that will help engineer development in the internal state.

In other words, we've noted that this is the development of civilization or higher levels of consciousness, for such was the format in which one gains access to the internality of their system; even as that was functioning alongside and separate all along. Yet, it is fairly uncommon to find the construction of a sociality that adheres to a dynamical system, rather than the easy formation of validation or other socialities which do not dynamically interfere with each other and ascent existential culpability.

There is a constant contention that is made available when there is a dynamical function between individuals, and this would not be something that parental figures would agree. Instead, the easier function of validation and meager reciprocity that has no bearing on internal movement, so that the finality of the product or subject is of little consequence.

As well, we can say that sociality degrades alongside the unavailability of internal movement and the stagnation and stubbornness of its contentious experiences. In this matter, we can say that the evolutionary process definitely required such a system, but it was also the willingness of individuals to ascertain an experience of contention, thereby continuing dynamical exchange for the finality of that development.

We could say that there were social groups, far and few between, that are of the second disposition, in which they merely validated each other and did not provide that dynamical system—and thus they have not made it into the pages of history, unless that is, they are a research subject for historical individuals.

Separation in Conflict & Trauma Processing

In mediation, one constantly navigates perceptual conjectures. Direct engagement is vivid but unstable. Effective processing often requires separation—mirroring how conflict resolution happens more clearly outside the moment. We know this in social affairs very well—in which, when an individual is in conflict with another, the understanding of that interactivity is only beneficial in its development when separate from the occasion, both emotionally and physically. Therefore, the first ongoing process of mediating conjectured interactivity is through the separation of that very interactivity itself, which can be difficult due to how salient and volatile the interactivity is, as we've noted in the case of confinement or other dreads of life.

PART III: REDUNDANCY, MULTIPLICITY & REPRESENTATIONAL LOOPS

Redundancy and Access: The Psychosocial Logic of Imitation

We may think of redundancy as a repetitive pattern—one that might seem immaterial to consider redundant as each step in the sequence is part of an overall pattern. While that may be true, redundancy also appears as a psychological experience and a process of reality that retains a certain reciprocity of information in a cyclical form, disrupting psychic expansion into formation. We can view redundancy as the imitation or reproduction of source material. The *thing* itself is what it is, and its copy formation is similarly imitative and redundant. For the *thing* is already itself; thus, what becomes an imitation cannot be the *thing* itself nor anything else, as it depends on the parameters of imitating that *thing*. Its only relevance lies in ascertaining the direction toward the *thing* itself. Once the *thing* becomes immaterial, any imitative sequences will also fall into oblivion.

We may notice that most aspects or phenomena are imitative of other phenomena. For instance, the transition between two locations, mental states, relations, or any other transitional period is a state of imitation within

The Structure of Consciousness

this redundancy. In the state of transport, it does not pertain solely to the origin or the destination—both are considered the occurrence itself—while the transition is not a *thing* in itself but rather imitates both points in a converging manner.

In fact, anything can be redefined as possessing an imitative property relative to something else. We eventually reach a universal formation that can be considered the *thing* itself rather than merely a sequence leading to another *thing*, and any further endeavor merely produces a confusing understanding of reality. Only well-developed social acceptance might interchange to a higher level of universality where that which was considered *jargon* yesterday can become the next *thing*, though we ultimately reach a limitation by remaining centered in our individuality and its strict parameters.

Once we have established that redundancy is found throughout nature and psyche, we can remove any distaste for its formation. Although everything may be imitative, not all phenomena are redundant. If the imitative aspect is used as a direction toward the *thing* itself—serving as a platform in a distinctive role—it is imitative but not redundant. It becomes redundant only when we cannot identify a purposeful objective in using the imitative platform to access the *thing* itself, due to various factors.

One such factor is the proximity between the imitative property and the *thing* itself. When it is too near or too copy-like of the substance material, it does not allow for a directive engagement toward the *thing* itself because its similarity prevents the necessary separation for access. At the same time, if the imitative properties are too distant and not distinct enough, there is no natural formation for direct access toward the *thing* itself, as it fails to evoke the usual social reality of such a course. Only through analysis does one recognize that it is the imitative property as it relates to the *thing* itself that, within regular sociality, becomes redundant.

Another factor contributing to redundancy is the existence of enough imitative platforms at present to access the *thing* itself so that a new platform offers no additional advantage. This is a structurally congruent situation, akin to having too many doors to a building that a new door becomes unnecessary. When the structural setting changes and existing "doors" no longer work properly, an extra access point becomes necessary and thus non-redundant.

This aspect is convoluted by its constant shift between redundancy and non-redundancy. The first factor is based on a fixed parameter of what is near and what is distant—and is fairly definable based on sociality and

Redundancy and Access: The Psychosocial Logic of Imitation

informational material—we might say that what is distant remains so unless a major change in sociality or psychic understanding occurs. Conversely, if today there is a multiplicity available to access the *thing* itself and tomorrow that access diminishes or those entry points become distractive, then a new sequence for access in the *thing* itself would become necessary and non-redundant.

Similarly, if there is little unfilled access to the *thing* itself apart from a single aspect, then without delay a new multiplicity may emerge to engender additional access. In this way, one gains the advantage of participating in the *thing* itself or the potential that underlies these imitative properties, rendering any new form of access redundant, as soon as the original source material is fully gained. When access to a *thing* itself is provided or sequenced in an instant, the market of imitative properties may lose the substantial nature of its structure, even if those properties demonstrate great competence. Thus, competence for potential surpasses competence for mere imitation.

Individual and Collective Choices in Shaping Redundancy

Another element in determining whether something is redundant or non-redundant arises from the individual or group interest in source material retrieved through a given medium. Although there may be multiple avenues for accessing source material, if an individual or group—especially one representing public interest—decides to use a particular structure as the medium, it would be the case that what would seem redundant for being a multiplicity will now gain access for the very choice of using that structure as a medium for access of the source material. Meaning to say that the choices of conceptual frameworks in setting aside and choosing a specific pathway of imitative material towards the source material, would be the case of gaining the formation of non-redundancy because of those very choices.

It could have been the case that there was multiplicity and thus these domains or aspects are redundant but because of individual or group choices, they become non-redundant and the rest of the multiplicity becomes redundant. It is the advantage of a change in social interest, which would have a medium to the source material become non-redundant, all the while others redundant only because of that very choice of access. The reason for choosing such over another could be nuanced or could be non-complex, for instance geographical proximity, or availability of access from the beginning. It could also be the case that it is a complex nuance, which allows for this choice, less common than the arbitrariness of the mediums based on what materializes for a serial moment in time and place. We often attribute this to fate, as it does not conform to a predictable or sequential structure; fate directs attention to a specific time and space differently than any other and it is not based on psyche development henceforth.

The Interplay of Zero & Redundancy in Existential Systems

The problematic aspects of redundancy (as noted) will only affect the locale or individual who has sought a sequential pattern of direction in which redundancy diminishes personhood accordingly. If the individual or locale does not engage in advancement with exponential growth, then the multiplicity will simply be an addendum to their mainstay of personhood. The point is that multiplicity is not a state of being but rather a manner of perspective, for the entire engagement is not linked to internal drivers. When the engagement is meant to include the wholeness of personhood, the experience of multiplicity becomes a mathematical division of personhood. (It is important to note that zero in standard mathematics is not simply "nothing" or a renunciation of another number—it is the unique additive identity, for every number a, $a + 0 = a$ and $a \cdot 0 = 0$.) This is not only critical in numeration but also in existential systems.

When we multiply zero, we diminish the entire attempt at multiplicity and return to the confinement of zero. (Just as any number multiplied by zero yields zero, one might metaphorically describe how, under certain conditions, a multiplicity of individual "identities" or experiences can be absorbed into an undifferentiated whole.) The very attempt to reach—through the wholeness of number (that is, zero)—into the possibility of existential movement without the buffer of another number causes the multiplicity to become an immediate division that turns to zero once again. However, the second zero, after the fact, is not the same as the first, because there was a strenuous reach toward what is beyond it. Therefore, it becomes a definitive zero instead of a standing zero. This means that although the wholeness of personhood during an existential movement has developed to be multiplicity causes one to be diminished to their prior state—as if no movement had occurred—there will still be an unrealized loss to the original state, with the potential of being perceived as a zero.

This is similar to the process of self-consciousness. If there is no consciousness, there is no self-reflection of that expansion. However, if there is consciousness, then the individual can self-reflect and become self-conscious, which only makes them realize the state in which they were always—like zero—while also acting as a major catalyst for change due to the consciousness beckoning that awareness. (While it is intriguing to use the mathematical properties of zero as a metaphor for existential states, one must distinguish between the precise arithmetic rules—such as $a \cdot 0 = 0$ uniquely—and the metaphorical idea that multiplicity or self-consciousness "collapses" into a single state.)

While there could be an argument for the benefit of self-consciousness—for the awareness it affords—it is generally assumed to be a negative provision. This is because the individual does not have the capability to engender change based on that awareness; it is rather an imposition without justification. Moreover, it is not a necessary movement of consciousness, but only what has been imposed by the environment, without the justification that this is the proper momentum for development. The entire episode of self-consciousness would leave the individual in a perpetual state of decline, even if their state remains unchanged, solely due to the reception of that awareness—which highlights the entity that exists. (Just as zero acts as the baseline for all number systems, *self-consciousness* in this framework operates as a critical point of reference, one that does not lead to movement but rather to a state of static awareness.) We could even perceive the episode as the diminishment of that very entity, for at least for a moment, we have a consciousness expansion that sacrifices the individual by recognizing the entirety of its entity and dispelling its composition.

We acknowledge that it is an abandonment, for an environment that engages in consciousness expansion does require individuals who

The Interplay of Zero & Redundancy in Existential Systems

experience a state of self-consciousness. If we find an environment in which not a single individual experiences self-consciousness, then we can identify that setting as lacking consciousness. This is a moot point, because it is the self-conscious individuals who propagate the momentum and vitality of that locale. Having endured a form of renunciation in their ashamedness and disruption of personhood, consciousness does radiate—usually embodied by those who attach themselves to that expansion. (This can be compared to zero, as zero is not just a placeholder, but it is what enables the differentiation between, for example, **10** and **100**—in other words, without zero, we would fail to recognize the power of numbers.)

This can be said in a similar vein to zero. Although multiplicity serves only to cast light on the very entity of zero, there is still the building of all numbers and their vitality that rely on zero. If we do not have zero, we do not recognize the power of numbers, because there is no other number to propose its production. We could say this is true only for multiplicity, but all other formulas are based on multiplicity. For example, addition is the conjecture of two numbers, but what good is the sum of two numbers unless we know what they confer? With multiplicity, we do not need to question why the multiple occurred, because it is self-evident that multiplicity follows from the redundancy of a singular entity.

Addition does not provide information about the two numbers; why would one number need to be included in another if all numbers arise from the expansion of one? For example, we would not add the number of siblings a family has unless we are concerned with a relational element regarding the father. However, we would follow the multiplicity of the generational lineage without needing to trace the ideation of the father, for it is implicit in the research. If you are following generational growth—hence multiplicity—we have already agreed to follow the expansion of the source.

The same can be said for subtraction, where we are only concerned with the decrease in sibling count because of the conceptualization of the family's source. Therefore, zero may not be the backdrop of addition or subtraction because they are not fundamental mathematical operations. Rather, zero becomes fundamental when realizing the source of a formula, so that we cannot have multiplicity without the backdrop of zero. For the very power of reflection—where the attempt at multiplication results in the generation of zero—gives credence to its regulation and control over the source, even to the extent of disrupting the entire endeavor of zero and sending it back to its propositional state.

This is why zero is included in all numbers as a placeholder for its multiple value. It is more than a placeholder; it is the recognition that a number is more than 1–9 because of its multiplicity, and nothing changes despite whatever extension we may attempt to make. Zero is the renunciation of the "1" in "10" by giving itself entirely as a self-conscious embodiment of that potential of multiplicity, thus assisting us in realizing that it is a ten rather than a one.

Self-Consciousness and the Cycle of Multiplicity

The point is that redundancy is not implicit in direct diminishment but rather serves to facilitate the realization and reflection upon the entity itself, in order to arrange something more. When one engages wholeheartedly in an environment of conscious expansion—and does so in a redundant manner—they become the zero for that potential, allowing it to be realized through multiplicity, whereas individual self dissolves. Without zeros in consciousness expansion, we are left with singular whole numbers that align with the idea of expansion, yet merely represent its potential rather than the act of propagating itself.

To expose, consciousness must rebound upon multiplicity and return to the whole number. The whole number can be represented by an individual who retains a distinct thread of consciousness—true for every advanced life form. The environment will orient itself around the highest whole number, while the rest become zeros, enabling that expansion to unfold.

This concept is better grasped in the realm of self-consciousness. Self-conscious individuals are not deficient in consciousness, but rather exhibit a deficiency relative to its permeation. Any retention of consciousness is automatically mirrored and achieved within expansion, so self-reflection falls upon the entity that has yet to have been subsumed by the masses of multiplicity. These individuals are self-conscious because they witness the vanity of their own entity, all beside a consciousness that has not integrated into their process. They cannot perceive the entity that has already managed a level of consciousness, as it has been canceled by multiplicity and thus appears as a redundant marker—a zero sum.

Where there is redundancy, there is multiplicity; and where there is multiplicity, there is a zero sum. The entity of multiplicity is inherently redundant—it cancels and propagates simultaneously. Multiplicity expands through redundancy and then contracts into a zero sum, for movement along

The Interplay of Zero & Redundancy in Existential Systems

the continuum is unending. Each particle or element is identical, and therefore highly volatile—expanding and contracting with momentous speed. Contraction occurs through renunciation, which renders the *whole* into a zero sum, accompanied by the experience of self-consciousness. Expansion then resumes through that very contraction.

If one were to observe their psychological state during self-consciousness, they would notice that it's not streamlined but marked by a constant oscillation—an attempt at expansion (which grants pensive power), followed by contraction, which dismisses them from the occasion, leaving the whole number as the solitary entity of perceptual worth. In this process, selfhood becomes a sacrificial conjecture. Until one musters the effort to become nuanced in consciousness—expanding in pursuit of an equal or greater claim to awareness—they remain categorized by their multiplicity and redundancy, once again forewent for the sake of the whole number.

In this way, consciousness becomes reflective by virtue of multiplicity and redundancy, within which everyone, at different times, serves as the sacrificial element that provides the zero sum—and with it, the coveted possibility of becoming the whole number.

Redundancy and its Role in Multiplicity

This is why it is important to retain the possibility of self-consciousness in an environment. When it becomes too secluded from self-consciousness, it loses its zero status and becomes an unrelated whole number, no different from any complex life form in the discretion of their subjective consciousness. Nevertheless, if there is too much engagement, then the expansion is now in elevation without a whole number to occupy the peak locale and obtain that sacrificial aim.

For renunciation is not performed by the whole number, as most assume, but by the process of multiplicity and redundancy itself. We can provide as many zeros as possible in an equation without the need to add a whole number, wherein the expenses are made so as not to be absorbed by a whole number.

This is why the primary role of individuals in an expansion system is to recognize the redundant detriments and find their proper justification, and to move toward a non-redundant essence or locale so as to both avoid being sacrificial and to become the whole number that receives the sacrificial expansion from other self-conscious individuals. We can view it as a sort of depressed conjecture in which renunciation can only be achieved once

The Structure of Consciousness

we fully recognize the value of zero and reflect back upon it with clarity. Only then will we become a whole number.

However, we can determine that it is a tragedy to partake in self-conscious expansion in an environment where there is no tenable reception—and where complete renunciation is not only redundant but also purposeless. This will be noticed by an individuals' subconscious, which will find the worst outcome of their process, rendering them redundant, sacrificial, and purposeless with no recipient. It is an automatic process, so it is upon individuals to become non-redundant and consequently the recipients and representations of that expansion, which occurs without awareness of who has developed to be the whole number.

The subconscious will acknowledge if there is a distinct recipient for the renunciation; because it is sensitive to forfeiture, there is a constant lookout for the recipient of its pensive propagation. They notice this in the process itself: when they expand in multiplicity and then contract through renunciation, they will either experience self-consciousness through an output similar to that during propagation—comparable to a signal that lacks a receiver.

The source of the signal will notice the similarity of the wavelengths, so it can be assumed that it has not been selected by a whole number. However, when the signal is picked up—although they are sent into the renunciation den of self-consciousness—they will receive that provision through an awareness that it was received as an alternative wavelength. In this manner, there is a resolution in the knowledge that it has served a higher purpose, thereby alleviating the experience of self-consciousness. Furthermore, they gain access to the psyche and mindset of the whole number, as their updated wavelength reflects not total renunciation, but partial renunciation—where they have relinquished certain elements and acquired others through a real and justifiable social exchange.

Representational and Genuine Systems of Consciousness

There will always be a representational whole number and a genuine whole number, and they will be differentiated because of the structure of consciousness. The representational objective is not to serve the essence of the real number or any difference, but to clarify that this process underlies the system. One must adhere to the positions in this linear structure. The necessity of a continuing representational model exists because, even though there is a subconscious system that underlies the representation, it requires a political formation for its actualization. In other words, without the representational model, the subconscious system will fade away, and vice versa. The positions of those in the genuine system will acknowledge the need for the representational model and will succeed in following those political aspects to gain access to their realm.

This is where the most significant reciprocity occurs between socialization: that of the representational whole number and the genuine whole number. This does not need to manifest in a political format, as long as both defer to each other for the necessities provided by them. We notice that political heads of state, corporate leaders, or leaders of major organizations will find themselves at a loss if they do not gain entry to the genuine whole number. When a representation lacks a connection to its source, it begins to take the power of socialization without considering the consciousness system. This creates a distinct disparity between systems, causing individuals to become rogue agents of social movement who deviate from the consciousness system.

Similarly, the consciousness system faces the same dilemma. If the genuine whole numbers deviate from the representational aspect and, thus, the political, they retain the consciousness leadership simply by acquiring the whole number. But they do so without correlation to the actualized and political system. They can only maintain that position by relying on the experience of representational effects, despite their deviation from its development. When such individuals participate in the consciousness system, they do so with leadership that seeks to overturn the current system to align with their constituents' parameters. This leads them to propose that the current structural and representational environment is fundamentally flawed and, therefore, deserving of radical change and redistribution. They do not do this consciously, but because they take the leadership of the whole number devoid of social exchange, especially to the representational agent of the same stature, they begin a leadership whose primary objective is to dismantle the current representation as they have proven that it does not align with consciousness.

We can even solve a societal problem using this method: either the representational whole numbers fail to maintain a coherent exchange with the genuine whole numbers, or the genuine whole numbers fail to maintain an attachment to the representational format for its actualization and respective recognition. An organization can be perceived in this way, where the representational aspect is the actualized organization and its echelon of leadership, with the consciousness continuum coinciding with its system. For actualized leaders are not those who retain the whole number in its real sense, but only in representation. We find it possible that the representational leader and the genuine whole number can exist in the same individual; however, this is more likely not the case. Potential must be differentiated because, even though an origin emanates from a potentiality that is usually based on the constitution of an individual, the current retention of the genuine whole number is not the potentiality of the system.

We acknowledge this in other contexts, even with the common phrasing that an individual 'retains potential', with the connotation of not participating in any system with that aspect. Even actualized potential is only the realized constitution of a system, and following that constitution only reaches the objective of its tenant. The consideration of consciousness embedded in the system and its sociality is absorbed by a stagnant constitution or its expansion as it follows those objectives. There is a conscious sentiment found in the process of actualizing potential, but that is only one of many considerations in a consciousness system. Therefore, it is not the case that the leader of an organization holds more than the constitution and its potential. The possibility of that potential is dependent on the consciousness system.

For example, if the genuine whole number positions against the constitution and the representational leader, it will be at the expense of the entire organization. The stream of consciousness will, as its first objective, restructure the entire representational model to follow the sentiment of that individual. Usually, an individual who retains the whole number of an organization that defers to the constitution and its potential will find it difficult to continue in such a model and will leave that organization. However, in the political case, the organization is comprehensive enough to include all other systems. So, if one were to obtain the whole number of that system and defer to the representational model, the system would be streamlined to fade and decline until a replacement is found. Unless, of course, they deviate from the political forum and its geographical control, in which case they will not retain the whole number, for there is no existential exchange between them.

The process of the representational retention of the whole number is through political acquisition, which is the actualized appearance of the system or organization. They represent the system, not to provide public communication, but as the head of the body for all internal constituents. They retain that superiority by virtue of their excellence in representational factors which cannot simply be attributed to power. The continuance can identify a more likely candidate despite the power differentiation. Usually, positions of power and representational leaders are the same but have gained access through different methods. For some, it can be a case of social recognition by virtue of the leaning of the multiples upon a singularity, and finding another with the agreement of the multiples; especially because this is a choice of consciousness, is difficult but not impossible.

Differing from the genuine consciousness system, where the multiples become submerged due to redundancy, and the whole number takes the unique and particular peak above redundancy, the representational model must endure this process in a political manner. Therefore, it must be the

The Structure of Consciousness

multiples who provide the renunciation of non-representational entities for all to converge upon a representational entity. Because of the nature of this renunciation, the only regulation is the agreement upon who the individual of representation is.

In the effect of the multitudes and their need for a candidate, the hierarchy of control or apparent power will lead to convergence. Once a multiplicity is engineered toward that convergence, others will follow suit, as they cannot diverge from the multitudes. When they attempt to do so, they will deviate from the system altogether and have a purposeless objection. The change in sentiment within that sociality can be attributed either to a shift in the perspective of power or to the fact that the representational aspect they embodied is no longer congruent with the current system. The ability of representation is based on the inclusion of the multitudes and the organizational structure. If the representation deviates from that appearance, they will be unlikely candidates. That shift of representation can occur arbitrarily, with a sentiment hovering above the individual that does not parallel the system.

Redundancy can be redefined as actualized interactivity against the backdrop of consciousness expansion that succeeds the individual. We would not say that the infantile state, which actualized interactivity, would be crossing the threshold to become redundant, because, in the effect of having no more access to a consciousness continuum than the interactive domain, they will actualize the entirety of their psyche. When that scope enlarges to include a more advanced consciousness continuum, the repetition to the interactive domain will be a deficit to greater development.

This should not lead to the conclusion that a child in an infantile horizon will not adapt to a broader consciousness continuum than that of the domain they inhabit. The child will participate in broader consciousness continuums, but they will remain aligned with their allegiance to the infantile interactive domain.

Structural & Conceptual in Psychological Experience

Most of our recent work has discussed the structural circumstances of the individual mind, viewing them as the normal setting, which allows us to perceive structural inference as the only criterion for regulation and process within the psyche. However, another process operates within the individual psyche that supersedes this requirement. Although bound by structure to some degree, it can function in a manner that transcends infrastructure's control. The psyche can do this because no structural mechanism dictates the concreteness of an element, alternatively its flimsy nature. Instead, it relies on a broader perspective—one that the structure itself cannot contain—for such an effect to take place.

For example, a room in a building may be considered a grand hall, but it becomes such only in its completeness, defined by its usage. There are structural elements—such as the first room upon entry, its size, and other characteristics —that shape the final appearance of a grand hall. Yet, the

The Structure of Consciousness

psyche can conceptually distinguish the room from the rest of the structure, besides altering its perceived distance from the entrance.

The door to the grand hall can be emphasized to a point where one may only see the inner space, no longer perceiving it as a "greeting" room. Moreover, one may envision the rooms beyond the grand hall as entirely distinct in character, not closely associated with the hall. As a result, for this particular awareness, the grand hall loses its defining character and becomes a space of limited effect in either direction. We acknowledge this in a palace, for its great hall does not act to the same effect because the quarters are distinctly separated—conceptually, serving as the external room of the palace rather than a meeting place for the internal system. In fact, the palace is in desperate need of an internal aspect to the great hall chamber, which, because of its conceptual separation, is difficult to conjure and maintain.

The same applies to psychological trauma. If one is penetratingly exposed to an experience in a specific space, such begins to act unlike its normal conceptual inference, becoming akin to a landmass where foreboding structural aspects lose relevance. However, the psyche does not partake with complete freedom in this process; it remains reliant on the structural footprint to some degree. A psychological trauma experienced in broad openness, for example, will be associated with the neighborhood or city, but in as much as structural references allow. If the experience occurs in a truly open space, then its association will extend only as far as the structural elements that define that openness. A trauma in the desert, for instance, will be linked to the entire desert—until a structural boundary, such as a nearby town or city, is reached.

To take this concept to its extreme, upon the moon, their experience encompasses the entire lunar surface, as no structural inference existed to limit the association to any specific part. The only associations present were in as much as the structure allowed, according to the experience. In open space, for instance, the experience would encompass the space in accordance with structural elements that define or halt that openness. Open space cannot be fully encompassed or marked with application unless there is a structural boundary, which defines it.

If the experience occurs in a proper desert, the entire desert becomes associated—until we reach a point where the desert ends, such as a town or city. To take this idea to its furthest extreme: when an individual stood on the Moon, it was the entire Moon upon which they stood, as there was no structural inference to limit or exclude any part of it. The Moon itself does not impose any constraint on that association, except for the structural inference of the ship. If the landing occurred without a ship, then the only structure would be the body and its apparel—and without attire, the body itself becomes the only structural reference for that experience. (This is to exclude those who are familiar with structural properties of the Moon)

Under normal circumstances, one regulates the psyche for the application of whatever structural inference to the chosen elements of the psyche. If one were to choose, they could format a profound experience in a structural locale and avoid another—even when the environment is fully engaged. For instance, in the case of a major celebration or gathering, the inference of placing psyche material upon that structural setting could lead to differentiate oneself by dictating the immaterial of the classification. One can simply notice their biological makeup and the individuality, which separates them from the environment, acknowledging that the environment is not a part of their integral makeup despite its prevalence.

It can be noticed that this setting is not an encapsulation of all social sophistication and endures its lacking elements, making for a stimulatory reality rather than an unreserved one. The psyche can differentiate, and in that differentiation, the surrounding experience will not affect them, seen as a fixed happenstance. The same can be said from the opposite perspective, in which the environment may be completely disassociated from enjoining in an experience, while the individual may participate with complete enmeshment—noticing all structural elements and their associations which lead to the most sophisticated aspects of society.

We are beginning to understand that, even as the average individual follows this same criterion—experiencing completeness within environments that do not fully support it, and avoiding immersion when the surroundings do—it is not an automatic experience. An individual possesses the key elements to control and regulate their choices, either participating in structural elements or avoiding them altogether.

This brings us to the central question: once one gains this control, where does one place the emphasis? What determines whether one engages or disengages from structural associations?

This brings us back to our previous works, where we examined in how there is a structural development that we can all agree leads to more socialized and societal inferences—and those that do not. A remote structural element does not espouse an association of urbanized sophistication, and even if the individual psyche tends to envision a deep

The Structure of Consciousness

experience within that space, it will only mark that structure more separated from its dependencies.

The same is true of a nondescript room within a structure, which can be turned into a conceptual haven of psyche depth, yet will not serve the entire structure—only because its structural reality is one of separation from the more prevalent spaces. This is why the restroom, despite its ability for psyche experience, will always be separated from the rest of the structure. If one were to download a depth experience in a restroom space, it would only formulate that location as distinct from the structure. This would not be true with the great hall, for if one does the same, the entire structure becomes associated with that experience, being the primary room of the structure.

These are no limitations of the psyche's participation, only the structural inferences which are separated to a certain degree and are afforded associations grounded by them. One can apply a recognition in how the restroom is structurally defined by the rest of the structure, taking note of how it is applicable to the whole. This will give the ability to associate beyond the restroom despite being inside its domain. However, the psyche, upon dwelling outside the restroom with any experience at all, will notice the prevalence of the structure as a space for more active dwelling—thus discounting the restroom.

There is the possibility that the restroom can be considered an unequivocal locale of experience, but in its associated attempt to reach outside its domain, any inference in that locale will discount the restroom chamber as distance from the rest. One can instill into the rest of the structure in how it is dependent upon the restroom, in how it reaches to its domain and participates with the rest of the structure. Because of the biological inference of the utility of the restroom, that memory will constantly be instilled, to which a separation will always take effect.

A trauma experienced in the restroom space will not necessarily extend beyond its domain into the rest of the structure. Most notably, trauma experienced in the outward housing domain is usually not associated with the restroom. However, trauma can extend beyond the restroom domain in the case when one becomes acutely aware of the structural connections between rooms beyond normal. Any time spent outside that room will assert a differentiation from the restroom.

This leads us to the premise that there are two coinciding aspects of consciousness that work hand in hand, yet are predominantly the domain of the conceptual framework. The first is *structural consciousness*, and the second is *conceptual consciousness*. Similar to the psyche, both require conceptual inference for the revealing of the psyche's contents and structural associations. The psyche needs structural association because it requires containment within parameters; without it, the psyche would not be instilled and would instead dissipate, lacking differentiation.

This applies on an individual level. However, there is a broader permeation of conceptual data based on structural competence, which works in tandem to produce the final result of the primacy of consciousness. Structural competence cannot be envisioned as the perfect connection, but rather as a conceptual permeation that functions within a reasonably competent structural system. It is the grouping and social sphere of conceptual reciprocity, at an advanced level of exchange, that is typically the determining factor—not the structural habitat. However, a significant deficiency in the structural domain can inhibit associations of conceptual exchange.

Comparable to the restroom—despite its high internal competency—due to its structural deficiency as the lowliest room in the structure, any events that occur there will not permeate into the surrounding environment and will be isolated from societal effects. Even a highly competent gathering, in which conceptual exchange takes place, will be confined to its location if it lacks a structural connection—meaning that the gathering did not account for location's associations which would allow the conceptual data to expand outward. In such a case, the structural incompetence will prevent any continuation beyond the immediate space.

The psyche acknowledges structural incompetence, just as it recognizes any experience within the restroom to not actively extend beyond its domain. When an experience occurs in a structurally deficient location, the encapsulated event cannot permeate through the structural reservoir of external life, remaining "stuck" within that space. The psyche will not only prevent further associations outside that realm, due to a differential structural inference—it will also prevent the dissemination of the contents within the psyche itself. In being structurally deficient, the psyche acknowledges that whatever the experience, it is not a primary factor for dissemination, as it cannot extend into the perceptual realm.

Immediately upon exiting this structural space, the psyche is compelled to engage with a domain that cannot include the experience, allowing the psyche to disseminate the information without structural reference. This explains why consciousness is intrinsically tied to structural habitat: any formation of consciousness that occurs without a structurally effective

The Structure of Consciousness

setting cannot disseminate its information to the rest of the psyche or to the external realm. The internal realm requires structural inferences to process this information, which is impossible when one retreats to a structurally deficient space. As a result, consciousness experience becomes isolated within the psyche, creating a problematic system.

This leads to a discrepancy in individual consciousness, now differentiated by structural references. Consciousness remains stagnant within the psyche, attempting to reconstruct a structural realm that aligns with the consciousness experience. This marks the beginning of a psyche that seeks to build a new civilization. In the absence of an existing structural system, and with encapsulated consciousness, the psyche attempts to create the first city—to construct a habitat and structure suited to this developing consciousness. However, since civilization already exists, the psyche will begin to build in opposition to the established structures, creating a foundation rooted in offence toward what appears to be a competent structure, yet proceeding as though it does not exist. This new structural creation will be deficient, much like the beginning of civilization, requiring a considerable amount of time and diversity to style progress within such an environment.

Therefore, the inevitable result of standalone consciousness is that one will begin the construction of a structural system—at least conceptually—which assumes the void of civilization, where they are the first members to prepare the system. Standalone consciousness does not wish to remain isolated and will seek to resettle. However, because of its structural deficiencies at the start, it will work to construct one, further distancing itself from existing civilization.

Another key element in the consciousness experience is proficiency. Even with structural competence, the social dimension of consciousness progresses through interaction. This progression does not rely on structural references but rather on the "moving conversation," where the reciprocity of consciousness uncovers new depths of reality through sociality. One can reveal a deeper reality from the consciousness experience, but this will once again lead to standalone consciousness, as the information cannot be integrated structurally. The social environment may not yet be aligned with the premises.

Representation, Interaction, and Physicality

There are three methods in interacting with a conscious environment or substance. The first method is interaction, the second, representation, and the third is physical.

[1] Interaction can be defined as a predetermined awareness of the full scope of the consciousness spectrum, allowing free rein and experience, which will always be tied to a physical location and its representations. In each of the cases and each of its coinciding methods, there will be a conciliation with the other two, but there is a dominant trait.

[2] Representations are the experience of conscious substance as most relevant to be described in an educated form. It displays itself as the informational realm that makes consciousness understandable. It is the dialogue pertaining to consciousness and is the forms of progression and innovation related to it. Yet, what represents itself also has a manner of

The Structure of Consciousness

interaction in addition to its physical ramifications that underpin its property.

We have mentioned in other works how representations must adhere to some physical manifestation—when they become unlinked, the representation begins to fade. Representations are the adulterated form of interactions, so that every representation will be noted for how it links back to preliminary interactions. Alternatively, interactions are preliminary forms of representation, so that one cannot interact with another unless there is some representation that gives credibility to that interaction.

With a complete dearth of representation, there is no ability for interaction because representation is the first step in the process of interaction. One cannot begin a preliminary conscious experience from the place of interaction but rather from the place of representation, which then allows for the availability of interaction. Although separate from representation, interaction is a partialization of that substance.

The process must go in a certain order. Since representation is the onset of any interaction, it must go first, and interaction must come after it. Without the dilution of representation toward interaction, one would not access the broad scope of their conscious habitation and environmental mappings that are not privy to direct representation.

[3] Physicality—or the oneness and unified nature of oneself to an infrastructure or locality—are the finality of the process. It is the concrete form that gives a certain acclaim and actualization to what precedes it. The major miscarriage of experiencing consciousness occurs when physicality is the first resort, so that one becomes unified without a proper inference of representations and interactions, which lead up to that unification.

Proper physicality, rather, perceives the unification as arbitrary but only as a quick means of realization between oneself and an infrastructure according to a domain that allows for synthetization. Immediately after that slender experience of physicality, one needs to depart so that they do not center on that physicality, ensuring that the unification does not become lost from its representational and interactive associations.

We can understand this more simply by way of an example. Sexual intimacy would not be proficient if it immediately went into the finality of the act of intercourse, devoid of foreplay or interaction, devoid of representation or sexual fantasy—only the immediate consumption of intercourse itself. The physicality—or the finality and purpose—of the sexual experience has been allotted only for itself in the procedure, so that

Representation, Interaction, and Physicality

it is lost to the fantastical realm that precedes it; or the nuanced and descriptive foreplay that dances between physicality and representation.

What is primary in a proper sexual interaction is representation, in which one enters into a fantastical realm of sexual ideas and its conceptual jurisdiction, so that when the activity becomes manifest, they have already performed the duty of creating a landscape in which this physicality occupies. However, if it is simply the representation that leads into activity, it would not be wholesome, for it lacks the interaction.

It might be more transparent to explain physicality as localized interaction. The psychological experience of becoming physical or participating with one's bodily functions within an infrastructure is such that the interactions of the psyche, at the moment of that process, will engage with the infrastructure without an awareness of wholesome consciousness. Whatever the permeating thoughts, they will become attached to that physicality, so that one engages with their interactive aspects within such infrastructure in a manner very specific and distinct from other infrastructures and especially from all availability of consciousness.

The reason this occurs is that one may naturally have interactive movement in their psyche, but because there is physical activity, that interactive substance becomes attached to that infrastructure, unified only in the manner of that specific interactivity.

For example, if one is agitated but performs physical activity with such state of mind and does so in a unified manner, the localized aspects of that physicality will become committed to that agitation. As a result, agitation is no longer just a state of mind—it becomes the reality structure of that physicality, so that one has a perceptual experience of agitation which becomes evident.

Instead of interactivity becoming a part of the equation, the entire reality structure becomes siphoned into that specific physical parameter, and such will only include the agitated state of mind. One can then be assumed to be the complete embodiment of agitation—both within the psyche and within their perceptual experience of the external reality. That is to say, agitation is the only existence possible in any coherent part of their psyche.

Consciousness as a Reflective Mode

The case may be that consciousness requires personification or is already personified by the individual and thus requires to be regulated as a personification. Moreover, consciousness serves as a receptor for one's existential attachment; thus, if it arises from domestic material, it will emanate from that very element within the individual.

Consciousness is a reflective point because the personification—or the entire engagement—is individualized, making it a reciprocal aspect of a social dynamic. It must therefore be treated as a social reciprocation in which reflection is a natural circumstance.

We will discuss the reflective property to understand the makeup of consciousness, but more importantly, the receptive nature of its structure. Although we can perceive consciousness as a continuum of expansion that stems from a center linked with sociality and environments, the personal manifestation differs. For, according to the individual, consciousness is experienced as the *peak representation* of the social records that are part of their imaginative network. The social representation of consciousness interacts with the psyche and its portions in a regulating manner, where the noblest character holds the seedlings of all other contents.

Peak representation brands consciousness the honorable member of the individual's social stratum, thereby regulating the entire psyche. Just as consciousness, at its central locality, is the nexus state of reality for all its dependencies; within the psyche, consciousness assumes the landscape of the peak state of reality—becoming the dominant factor in the psyche's process. Because of this structure, the relationship with *peak consciousness* is of paramount importance. If it is wearisome, then the incorporation of *peak consciousness* will impose a wearisome state throughout the psyche.

This is similar to engagement with royalty—if one develops a resentful relationship, the royal namesake, which already embraces the status of a form of *peak representation*, will become a mirrored resentment upon all of social society, which is inextricably tied to them. Thus, resentment toward leaders manifests as a generalized perception of all sociality by means of that same resentment, by virtue of royalty being the peak of sociality.

The same is true of the psyche: consciousness is the topmost of its process. If a problematic relationship develops through it, then it becomes the very haven through which all mental contents are disseminated. Resentment, once embedded, becomes the nobility of the mind, with all its dependent contents constrained by those parameters. When *peak consciousness*, holding a resentful perspective, is incorporated into the psyche, it ceases to be merely a relationship difficulty—it becomes the entire foundation of consciousness itself. At that point, consciousness can only process reality through the lens of resentment.

The same applies to royalty—when resentment toward a distinct royal figure becomes the defining perception of royalty; it ceases to be just an aspect of the relationship. Instead, it becomes the symbol of crowned heads for any public representation. The relationship is then defined by virtue of royalty being an effectuated member of sociality that is related to all one's relationships.

When that relationship changes modes, one's interaction with all sociality evolves accordingly, because royalty functions not only as a relational figure but also as a conscious representation. If one can distinguish between the relationship aspect and the representational aspect, then a wearisome relationship will not affect the perception of representation itself. This is the case for kin of royalty, where the personal relationship is wholly separated from the representation of royalty. While resentment may exist on a personal level, it does not extend to the social function and dependency of royalty.

To successfully disperse the relationship from the representation, one must treat the relationship as a distinct modality, pertaining to non-

Consciousness as a Reflective Mode

representational activity, ensuring that it does not encroach upon representational aspects. History shows that royal kin have often lost this distinction, allowing relationship difficulties to bleed into the representational aspect. We can perceive the same phenomenon within the psyche: relationship-based resentment may not stem from a personal issue but from an aspect of representational activity in the mind. Recognizing this distinction helps one determine whether their engagement is personal or representational.

This also applies to *peak consciousness*, which retains both representational and personal activity within the psyche. If no distinction is made between representational and relational, then a failed relationship with consciousness becomes embedded in its representation—thereby affecting the entire psyche. This leaves us with two possible approaches:

1. Ensuring that any interaction with consciousness stems from a formative and stable relationship.
2. Separating the two domains—one for representation and the other for personal relationship.

We can illustrate these approaches through religion and secular manifestations. The religious approach seeks to separate representational from personal, engaging primarily with the personal relationship while relying on a universal domain for representation. The secular approach, on the other hand, confines the representational and the personal within the same domain but ensures that interactions focus on achieving a perfected relationship. If such is not possible, it disengages entirely.

Even within the secular approach, upon encountering *peak consciousness*, one must still develop a certain relationship. This is circumvented by engaging with consciousness for its representational properties while distancing from personal interaction—thereby avoiding its personal ramifications. While this method can function without immediate adverse effects, an inability to personally interact with consciousness results in one left to the mercy of arbitrary circumstances, without any control or regulation over consciousness itself.

The Regulation of Psyche through Conscious Interaction

The problem is such that if one's entire psyche depends on a representation not regulated by the internal psyche process, they lack control over their psyche's contents and processes—to the extent that they

The Structure of Consciousness

become entirely predictable. We only need to trace consciousness as it arises from an individual's external routines and context to understand their outcomes. Therefore, statistics can be used to predict both current and future processes. We only need to follow consciousness as it stems from its external routine and position such enclosed by that individual to determine all their outcomes. Hence, statistics can predict both future and current processes.

Therefore, one must personally interact with consciousness, as this grants the ability to regulate and control it—even though there remains the possibility of a problematic relationship. Consider royalty: one may engage with royalty from a representational standpoint, becoming an honorary member of the corporation without any regulatory influence. Or, one may interact with royalty in a way that grants access to reconfiguring it—though this runs the risk of creating a problematic representation, potentially straining the relationship itself.

A similar dynamic applies to a friend of a leader, who enjoys complete regulation over their representational figure but faces the adverse effect that, if the relationship turns irksome, the representational activity connected to their psyche—based on this sociality—will erode all their social connections. This holds true for all social stature: one may choose to engage from a representational standpoint or from an interactive one. If engagement is representational, the psyche's processes will be regulated according to that premise; if interactive, one gains equal footing with the figure. However, if the interaction becomes troubled, the representation one embodies will erode all the dependencies of the psyche.

This explains the troubling circumstance when a venerated figure is revealed to be morally degraded. A populace that engaged with such a figure only from a representational standpoint must now contend with moral depreciation across all dependencies of their psyche—compounded by the awareness of the cause of that depreciation, yet without any control or means of regulation. Had they engaged interactively instead, this moral depreciation would not have affected their psyche, as the effect is determined by the nature of interaction. Yet if the interaction itself becomes burdensome, so too does the representation, leading to a degradation of the psyche.

To prevent this relationship from going awry, one must engage with consciousness as if it were another person—one deserving of emblematic status—since it represents *peak consciousness*, capable of reflecting the entire contents of the psyche. This engagement is not merely an acknowledgment of consciousness, nor a requisite of early developmental stages, but a necessity, born of the human predisposition to personalize. Genuine interaction with consciousness requires a developed relationship—one that is upstanding and complete in its recognition of consciousness and its stature in relation to the psyche's contents.

Interaction with Representational Figures

The personification-estimation is based on the natural endeavor of personal projection, such that an individual might need not develop that personification if they do not notice the intricacies necessary for interaction. In other cases, it would require achieving a highly developed state of social interaction, as that is how one perceives the situation.

The regulation of interactivity is only necessary insofar as it pertains to the inclusion of personal aspects that truly manifest. When they do not, it is not required, for the representation is more than enough. The interaction with a representation serves only to provide temporary contextual direction for the dissemination of representational material, but it is not an interaction with the representation as an entity or persona. However, it is natural for an individual to interact with any substance as if it were another social entity, thereby necessitating that, at least as much as interaction occurs, there should be recognition of such and a determination to regulate it.

For an interactive composition, *peak consciousness* may very well be accessed through interaction alone rather than through representation. However, this is a fallacy, as the interaction itself is not true. Anyone engaging in the mode of interaction is still engaging aspects of the psyche that are representational, despite their preference for interactivity. It is akin to the relationship between a leader and close companion: while the connection may appear purely interactive, the leader's representational nature inevitably permeates the companion's psyche as a representational display, regardless of their insistence otherwise. Those who engage with a leader at a high level of interactivity typically maintain embodied interactive roles, ensuring that they neither access nor engage with consciousness —let alone *peak consciousness*.

A child's practiced position closely resembles this high level of interactivity, so their connection to parents usually manifests as an interaction with them rather than a recognition of the representational aspects of parental stature. However, this presents a danger for the child because, at the level of the psyche, the parental figure is encountered as a representational element, not as an interactive locale. By engaging with the

The Structure of Consciousness

parent, as it were purely interactive rather than representational, the child risks overexposing themselves to the regulatory and controlling elements of the psyche. With such an intense level of interactive engagement—yet without the buffering effect of representational activity—the child absorbs more from the parental representation than they can manage.

In the perspective of the child, the interaction is simply social exchange and a proper relationship, while the parental figure represents reality herself—for the child. The parent is not a relational figure and instead is the formation of all parameters for the child's psyche; hence representational. Therefore, the child becomes over-engaged in the parameters of reality and its representational regulation upon the contents of the psyche. The final outcome of this discrepancy is that the child's psyche will endure an over-interactive experience for the reason that reality is constantly providing more information to be transferred as interactive. In some sense, it is ironic because the child is only attempting to gain a semblance of interaction and instead, receiving a demanding quantity of interaction; cumbersome to ever handle.

This is the general problem of interacting with representational figures or entities, in which they become overstraining the psyche for their constant reinterpretation and figuration for the entire psyche landscape, causing interactivity of every element of the psyche and proportion to the change of representation.

Secondly, it becomes cyclical, for the psyche is interacting with the very generality of what provides interaction, so that in the interaction, it becomes a demand of a further interaction, which cannot be stopped. For in interacting with the representational figure they become the reality of the child's psyche, demanding itself to be interacted. With each continued interaction, the psyche descends further into a spiral of internal deterioration. As the interaction continues so does the downtrend state of a spiral interaction in the internal state of the psyche.

The fact of the matter is that the psyche can only engage properly with non-representational material; when it encounters representational material, all interaction becomes subordinate to that representation. Despite the prevalence or development of the interaction, it would only prove a more integrated representation, which would require the same reaction and interaction as one perpetuated towards it. Because one has the interaction towards the representational figure, which only represents itself to provide interaction, the reception of that interaction will be in accordance with the manner in which one interacts with it —only that it would become the basis of all thought instead of merely a single domestic thought in a pattern of interactivity.

In the usual case of interaction, one can engage with another figure so that it will be simply the material of interaction that is validated or dynamically interposed by the other figure. But when there are representational elements, the entire framework of reality develops to be surrounded by the interaction so that one understands the representation in accordance with how they fashion their interaction towards it. Then, when there is a reception of that reality framework, all there is left are those specific interactions that must be downloaded on a continual basis throughout the psyche's contents.

This is where we get a perpetual motion of the same interactive substance—the continuous mimicry of the interaction. The first interaction was genuine, but because it was approached through a representational figure or entity, it reciprocated that direct interaction as the forwarded reality framework, which then imposes upon the psyche and its contents, making it dependent upon the representation to fulfill that recognition and validation of interactivity. In some sense, the entire mind works as a loop to validate the interactivity, which is based on the representation, which in turn is based on the initial interaction that was genuine.

One cannot even disrupt the process or distinguish the representational adaptation as unreal or surreal because it is already an integrated framework that demands interactivity. The only method to halt the spiral interactive plunge is by separating the initial interaction. If we could direct attention to the obsessive compulsion of the specific interaction at its first point—when it was genuine—and detach from the representational figure or entity, we would find that the cycle stops. The entire vitality of the cycle begins because one seeks the interaction, so that in psychoanalysis, we will find it is usually compulsion based on an initial interactivity that one is reluctant to divest. Regular instances of interactive spirals will not be the cause of psychotherapy because, at some point, one will simply depart from the initial interaction, as there is no harm or trauma associated with the purposeful objective of that initial interaction. In most cases, it is merely a substance of interaction to provide material, and when that material proves unworthy, detachment occurs naturally.

We might venture from this premise that such an interaction with representational figures or entities is problematic from the onset. However, we will notice that individuals who assert such claims and continuously interact with a representational figure or entity do so merely by way of a representational effect—that is, as their own representation in its mirrored ensemble from the initial representation.

The personal basis is not included; rather, it is a reflection and mimicry of the representation, so that one is receiving while not integrating into that system. In this case, one will be at the mercy of the representational movements, as there is no addendum to counter or display specific social differentiation from the mimicry. The only choice in the matter is to which entity or figure the chosen representational aspect is given to—but not in proportion to anything beyond that. Instead, one becomes a true follower in that sense. Upon accepting a reality framework to be true and genuine — that is, accepting the representational entity as reality by associating and integrating that representation as the representation of the internal psyche state—the outcome is that one is no longer in leadership over their psyche. Rather, these representational inserts take on that role.

As a relational entity, they embody the very formation of all parameters governing the child's psyche—hence, they are representational. Consequently, the child becomes excessively engaged with the structural parameters of reality itself and its representational regulation over the psyche's contents. The result of this discrepancy is an over-interactive experience, as reality continually supplies more information to be processed as interaction. Ironically, in seeking a sense of interaction, the child instead receives an overwhelming degree of it—far beyond their capacity to handle.

This is the fundamental problem of interacting with representational figures or entities as they become overwhelming for the psyche due to their constant reinterpretation and restructuring of its entire landscape. Every change in representation alters the psyche's internal framework, forcing interaction with every affected element in proportion to these shifts.

Additionally, this process becomes cyclical—the psyche engages with the very source of interaction itself, creating an endless demand for further interaction that cannot be halted. By engaging with the representational figure, the juvenile's psyche internalizes it as reality, which in turn demands continuous engagement. As this cycle persists, it leads to a downward spiral of relentless interactivity within the psyche's internal state.

The Perpetual Loop of Representational Interaction

The matter of fact is that the psyche can only interact properly with non-representational material. When it engages with representational material, all interaction serves that representation. Regardless of how the interaction develops, it merely reinforces a more integrated representation, requiring

Consciousness as a Reflective Mode

the same reaction and interaction as was initially perpetuated toward it. Since one interacts with the representational figure—which itself exists solely to facilitate interaction—the reception of that interaction aligns with the manner in which one engages with it. However, rather than being a single thought within a broader pattern of interactivity, it becomes the foundation of all thought and perception.

In a typical case of interaction, one can engage with another figure in a way that allows the interaction to remain a mere exchange of material, dynamically mediated by the other figure. However, when representational elements are involved, the entire framework of reality becomes structured around the interaction. One understands the representation according to their manner of interaction with it, and as the framework of reality is received, all that remains are those specific interactions—continually embedded into the psyche's contents. This creates a perpetual motion of the same interactive substance, a continuous mimicry of the interaction. The first interaction may have been genuine, but because it was approached through a representational figure or entity, it reciprocated an interaction as a forwarded reality framework. This framework then imposes demands upon the psyche, which, being dependent upon the representation, must fulfill that recognition and such validation of interactivity. In essence, the entire mind functions as a loop, validating interactivity based on the representation, which itself was formed from the initial, genuine interaction.

One cannot easily disrupt this process by distinguishing the representational adaptation as unreal or illusory, because it has already become an integrated framework that demands interactivity. The only way to halt the spiral into interactive compulsion is by separating the initial interaction from its representational fixation. If one focuses on the obsessive compulsion stemming from that first genuine interaction and detaches from the representational figure or entity, the cycle ceases. The vitality of the cycle originates in the search for interaction, which is why psychoanalysis often finds that compulsions stem from an initial interactivity that one is reluctant to abandon. A normal interactive cycle does not lead to psychoanalytic concern, as one naturally departs from an initial interaction unless trauma or harmful fixation is attached to it. In such cases, the interaction serves merely as a medium for material exchange, and once that material loses value, detachment occurs naturally.

From this, one might conclude that interaction with representational figures or entities is problematic from the outset. However, those who make such claims often continue to interact with a representational entity solely through its representational effect. In such instances, they merely mirror the initial representation, without including any personal basis. Their engagement becomes a reflection and mimicry rather than an integrated system, leaving them at the mercy of representational movements. Since they contribute no counterbalance or differentiation from this mimicry, their only choice is to select which entity or figure will serve as their chosen representation. Beyond that, they exercise no control, effectively becoming followers of the representation. When one fully accepts a representational framework as true and genuine, integrating it into their internal psyche, the result is a loss of autonomy. Leadership over the psyche is forfeited, replaced by representational inserts that dictate perception and interaction.

Furthermore, individuals who operate purely within representational systems often lack the nuance and cognitive flexibility necessary to discern how representational aspects serve broader structures. Their grasp of representational material remains limited, as they engage only through the representation itself rather than through a meta-analysis of the system. As a result, they remain subject to environmental pressures and social intuitions, following representational frameworks without clear awareness of their underlying structures or hierarchical functions within consciousness.

Therefore, interaction with a representational figure or entity is necessary if one seeks to navigate the complexity of that representation. More importantly, it grants access to the process of representational internalization that occurs through such integration. Without personal engagement in this process, one will be unable to regulate or control the leadership of their psyche, remaining bound to an externally imposed reality framework with no means of self-governance.

Binary Requirement of Representational Interaction

"We see that a double requirement emerges: losing balance in such a structure results in either an interactive spiral or a loss of psyche leadership, which then becomes an incorporated representational activity over which one has fairly limited control. Another such strenuous aspect is the over-incorporation of representational activity that regulates and leads the psyche. In the usual case, the representational direction incorporated from mimicry on the outside has an effect, but it is rather subdued by the process of psyche contents, busy interacting with their sub-particles, so that leadership loses some ability, momentum, and liberation. Furthermore, in the case of mimicry, one is almost sensitive to the subject of that leadership because it is not their own and instead follows many advances in the interactive material of that representational assertion.

When one interacts with representational entities and its activity at a normal rate, on a normal basis, the result will be a high degree of integration of representational roles for the psyche, since there is a constant reintegration and reassertion. One is never truly at rest in the psychic process because the framework of reality is in constant motion. Similar to the child who seeks constant interaction with their parents, simultaneously incorporating the parental figures as statures to be embedded to their psyche, to the point that it is almost experienced as oppressive to the rest of psyche contents. Because there is constant dialogue between the interaction of the representational figure and the child, multiple frameworks of reality become incorporated as these dynamics develop. As a result, the psyche's parental representation is on high alert, constantly changing and demanding reinvigoration. (Superego) This is why parental figures who impose a high mode of expectation upon children usually find that the child's psyche development incorporates a singular, rigid representational figure—one they behold throughout their life. Although we could say that the expectation has created the impression at such a level, it does so without nuance, so that, as long as one meets the criteria—however limited and narrow—they find themselves freed from parental demands.

The other case is when parental figures seek interactive experiences and relationships at all times, demanding continuous interaction between parent and child instead of enforcing representational expectations. In this case, the child's psyche develops to incorporate a very complex and diverse parental entity for representation—one that compensates for the lack of clear demands by its sheer intricacy and complexity, leaving little room for deviation. Additionally, the child continues to utilize those parental figures as representational activity rather than for interactive experiences. While the parent may perceive their engagement as interactive, for the child, it is merely a performance of a more elaborate representational figure. The parent may then find themselves unable to communicate further representational demands because the representational element has become so integrated into the child's psyche that any additional expectation is perceived as more oppressive than the already overwhelming system.

The opposite is true of the parental figure who imposes representational expectations. If the parent increases their expectations and demands, it does not necessarily become more oppressive for the child, even if it appears so externally. This is because representation, in this case, remains in the realm of mimicry rather than complexity, allowing for some degree of psychic freedom, so long as the child meets certain representational parameters.

Thus, balance must be maintained. On one hand, interacting with representational figures and entities is necessary, as it provides a strict reality framework that is unquestioned and required for orientation. On the other hand, when representational interaction lacks nuance, one becomes trapped in an endless cycle, unable to regulate the integration of those representations. *The call to action* in such cases is to engage with representational aspects in a way that makes them more complex and nuanced, allowing for better regulation. Only through personal interaction with representations can one access and integrate proper representational aspects for the betterment of their system.

However, when representational complexity overwhelms the psyche — leaving no room for psychic movement beyond representational activity — the appropriate response is mimicry and adherence to established representational systems. In such cases, interactions themselves create excessive representational complexity, preventing the psyche from engaging in free exchanges beyond representational constraints. This results in a perpetual need to engage with *representation* in order to maintain any sense of psychic freedom. It is akin to a child who interacts excessively with parental figures to the extent that all other interactions become secondary. Instead of engaging with reality directly, they accept parental figures as simplistic representational icons, allowing them to process other psychic content without constant recalibration to the parental representation.

Encouraging a child to engage solely in mimicry and representational adherence denies them true interactivity. The reality is that parental interaction with children is based on a false premise—it is not genuine interaction but a structured representation parallel to what the child understands as beholden to be interaction. If a parent were to interact with their child in a wholly authentic manner, it would disrupt the representational dynamic. The parent, treating the child as an equal participant in interaction, creates an imbalance, as the child lacks the ability to reciprocate at that level. Instead, the parent reconstructs an interactive system that provides the illusion of interactivity, even though both parties are merely engaging in a representational exchange.

In all representational structures, there is an interactive dynamic between subjects and leaders—where the subject engages in mimicry and

Consciousness as a Reflective Mode

the leader performs their role within the representational system. However, this dynamic does not function as a direct exchange but rather as a structured, hierarchical interaction. The subject follows the mimicry of the leader, while the leader responds according to the structure of leadership. This is the foundation of interaction in real societal frameworks, and each party experiences it subjectively.

The same applies to the parent-child dynamic. The parent retains a dynamic exchange with the child, but it is based on a vast and complex internal framework that has little to do with the child's subjective experience. Meanwhile, the child progresses through life by interacting with parental figures and the surrounding reality framework gradually develop the ability to engage with these incorporations. The goal of the child's development is to separate interactive dynamics from representational ones, allowing for engagement with reality without constantly reverting to representation for validation.

When a parent reconstructs an interactive dynamic, they do so to provide the child with an accessible level of interaction—one that aligns with the child's cognitive framework. Another child may progress differently, not deviating from representational activity but instead engaging in deeper mimicry and nuanced adherence to shape their reality framework. While true interactivity may not be overt, it remains an underlying process—especially when retrieving information from the representational system. This interaction is performed so seamlessly that it appears as an adaptation rather than an integration. However, over time, as development continues, such interactivity becomes increasingly minimized, avoided in favor of maintaining the representational system without unnecessary deviation.

PART IV: COSMIC, POLITICAL & SYSTEMIC LOCALE

Cosmic Elements: Local Interaction and Social Agreement

The central locale and its eminence can be bonded by any contextual element, so long as it is not universal. Because it postulates itself as a naysayer of universality, the only instances in which true interaction occurs across the spectrum are cosmic events. These include seasonal changes, weather patterns, and celestial occurrences—phenomena that provide a shared experience for the entire populace without requiring a universal framework or availability.

One of the earliest major sciences, arguably the primary, can be attributed to this interaction: astrology. In its cosmic concern, astrology precludes rather than excludes any constituents on Earth, since all are composed of natural ingredients. Although it stretches the limits of cosmic nuance, astrology serves as an interactive mirror —especially when considering its direct relationship with individuals through weather patterns and celestial events. It thus allows for interaction despite being localized despite the fact that it appeals as a global occurrence.

The historical development of astrology has been diluted, reduced to the universal reality of its process and its parallels to individual experience—

an outcome dictated by societal choices. Even cosmic events are considered only in relation to their chosen attribution within contextual interaction. Based on this selection process, certain cosmic events can become polar opposites of their original stature; for instance, night may take precedence over day due to shifts in societal perspective. While some attribution to day and night remain a universal experience, the direct significance of these elements is determined by the populace and, in particular, by the central locale.

This dynamic binds the central locale to its primitive state, which cannot deviate significantly from universal cosmic elements except in ways that allow for redirection, subjugation, or subversion. Despite the capacity to regulate and control individual experiences in relation to weather patterns, weather patterns themselves remain one of the most prevalent interactive bases for the central locale.

Even as seasonal changes have departed from their agricultural roots, they continue to serve as dominant interactive perspectives for the central locale. If any other interactive basis besides cosmic adaptability and change were available, it would have been revealed by now. Instead, we must assert that no possible deviation exists because these elements remain the most notable and universal without reverting to individual or societal constructs.

Adaptability and change serve as pivots for this interaction because they are consistently demonstrated through contextual redefinition, reinforcing their own definition. This is why either the beginning of night or the beginning of day is among the most prevalent interactive experiences—each providing a shared definition acknowledged by all individuals.

Celestial Adaptability and Individual Experience

Even with the complexity of weather patterns, cosmic events, and celestial adaptability, not all such occurrences are universally included in the populace's experience. Only those that can be demonstrated in a simplistic and universally comprehensible manner achieve broad agreement and interaction.

Because celestial adaptability is the only contextual interaction with universal proportions at the central level, individuals may follow this proposition too thoroughly, even to their detriment. When a weather pattern produces prolonged rain, one may lose traction in the interaction yet lack the ability to disengage, as it appears to be the only substantial interaction. However, it is merely society's proclamation that allows this prevalence to take effect; they should not be considered the only interactive elements.

Cosmic Elements: Local Interaction and Social Agreement

Additionally, their opposites must also be acknowledged—rain can propose itself as a non-rain element, just as other celestial events, though less immediately impactful on individual experience, provide adaptability and redefinition that rain does not.

For example, during a period of rain, an equinox may occur, offering a different pivot of adaptability and interaction. While an equinox may not be as immediately perceivable as rain, its universality and role as a recognition platform to provide nuance. Thus, two themes emerge, the prevalence of individual experience in relation to cosmic events such as rain and the universal agreement on events that, though less impactful on individual experience, maintain significance due to their universal stability.

An individual can avoid rain by seeking shelter or residing in an environment where it is absent. However, an equinox cannot be avoided by a single individual—it cannot be perceived and ignored indeed must be agreed upon if proposed. The alignment of Saturn and Jupiter is a universal cosmic event, but it is neither experienced individually nor widely agreed upon unless society deems it significant. If, for any reason, it becomes a propositional event that society focuses on, it will gain prominence as an interactive experience but will lack the culpability of the standard equinox, as it does not provide individual experience.

Cosmic Balance and Conceptual Interaction

Cosmic elements possess a rare advantage: the ability to balance conceptual attachment. A conceptual interaction can drive the pursuit of a reality structure that moves beyond the fluidity and habitat of reality itself. Because of this, the conceptual platform must have the capacity to rebalance itself.

Nature's elements offer this opportunity on a grand scale. Days are balanced by nights, seasons by other seasons. The moon serves as a sign of equilibrium, its presence countering extreme weather patterns, just as water patterns regulate each other. We often perceive these dynamics as cycles, but they can also be understood as balancing extremes. If one engages conceptually with the Sun, the Moon remains a constant reflection point, reminding us that any perception is merely one side of a coin. Even when rebalancing occurs, the responsibility ultimately falls on the individual to complete the process. A historical tradition that deifies the Sun, for instance, lacks nuance without the Moon as a point of inflection and reflection.

However, in a deep, dynamic relationship with nature's elements, one inevitably reaches an abyss where rebalancing forces take effect. Those who romanticize the Sun—following its patterns and extreme conditions—will ultimately reach a precipice where the Moon's luminescence commands attention, offering a departure from the Sun's dominance. When one pursues a dynamic inference to its fullest extent, even a deeply cultivated love will eventually turn inward, shifting from a conceptual landscape to a self-defined position. In cases of codependency—where love is mistaken for an absolute reality, excluding the possibility of reclaiming selfhood—the dynamic inference remains unexplored. The absence of contrast prevents the opposite force from taking effect. Human relationships serve as the perfect offset for this balance. The very structure of a relationship contains the inherent pull back to individuality, ensuring that even within complex relational dynamics, the DNA of personhood remains intact.

By contrast, conceptual frameworks such as religion, politics, and education often lack this intrinsic balance. Beyond their failure to provide universality—since political ideologies do not encompass all of human nature, nor does education fully account for the breadth of intellectual and psychic experience—they also do not rebalance themselves. An educational subject, for example, can be extended indefinitely without any built-in mechanism to reassess the full scope of intellectual possibility or the human experience that encompasses these elements.

A social relationship can be claimed as evidence of the universality of individual experience, for there is nothing in such a relationship that remains exclusive to isolated parts of the psyche. Rather, it serves as a reflection of the wholeness of selfhood. Other conceptual frameworks do not offer this inclusivity.

This is the inherent problem with intellectual conceptual frameworks: they continuously fall into cyclical reasoning, never becoming fully aware of the broader intellectual or humanistic context in which they exist. The same applies to political frameworks, which, while they may expand, do not inherently dispel reality but instead serve as just one of many perspectives on it.

This brings us to the challenge required of conceptual frameworks—they must provide a manual rebalancing mechanism to counteract the extremity of their own perspectives. Additionally, they must incorporate an

Cosmic Elements: Local Interaction and Social Agreement

inference toward universal inclusion —of the psyche, of social structures, and of nature itself.

To achieve this, one must mirror the process of celestial interaction. For example, if a conceptual framework such as religion is considered, it must be offset by an external celestial reference—akin to how the moon provides a necessary counterbalance—reminding us that religion is not the only perspective but rather a frame of reference. Secondly, conceptual frameworks must be aligned with universal relevance so that they do not remain solely religious perspectives but instead act as bridges to broader, universal elements—elements that may happen to find expression through religious literature. If we were to follow the nuanced data within these subjects, we would find that religious frameworks often function as coverings for universal perspectives. They do not exist merely for their own sake but instead provide a stable foundation from which further explorations of universal elements can emerge—elements that might have remained inaccessible without such initial structures.

For instance, religious frameworks have long associated water with public rituals. This association has, over time, contributed to the global recognition of water as a universal experience. Had religious traditions not emphasized water's significance, it might have been either delayed in recognition or entirely overlooked as an essential element of human experience.

Domestication and Reality

One of the most primary and essential conceptual frameworks is domestication, specifically in the realm of the family body. This arena of domestication serves as a conceptual framework that allows for the experience of specific data points that do not align with wholesome reality but must be engaged with in an embodied sense. Therefore, it is within this domain that we require an offset, ensuring that one does not perceive or believe that domestication is reality itself.

Domestication has the most pressing tendency to be perceived as reality itself and is the most concerning in the two requirements mentioned. There is no inherent offset to domestication, only a manual recognition that it must not serve as the ultimate end of all interaction. Additionally, there is no recognition that domestication expands toward universality; rather, it appears far from it. This is why domestication is the domain most in need of manual input—it does not possess the mechanisms for automatic correction. If left unattended, domestication will naturally upend the

The Structure of Consciousness

individual by presenting itself as the only presumed reality, devoid of universality.

The manual process of offsetting domestication can be accomplished by recognizing its stature—how it neither informs on reality itself nor displays the entire scope of reality. Another method is to interact with domestication within conscious expansion, allowing it to serve as an avatar or representation of that domain rather than mere simplistic domestication. We can observe slight offsets within domestication, particularly in sexuality, which follows cycles of stimulation and non-stimulation, such as the menstrual cycle. In such cases, domestication contains an internal offset, where the non-stimulatory phase serves as a separation from that domain. The same can be said for relationships, which also possess a dynamic cycle—engagement with that domain when necessary and, when not, an inference to dispel the illusion that domestication is reality or even close to it.

Domestication does not provide the orientation that all relationships do—the dynamic inference to selfhood, offsetting circumstances, and granting wholesome universality to one's system. Since domestication does not infer universality, its dynamic inference can be so misaligned with the individual's circumstantial reality that it becomes mere speculation in the dark, cut off from true reality. An individual who perceives domestication as a dynamic force that provides an agreeable picture of their stature is fundamentally lost in their environment. Furthermore, this dynamic inference does not provide an offset to personhood because it does not reach personhood; it remains bound to particular occasions of interest within domestication itself.

This is why romance and domestication are two separate affairs—the end of romance marks the beginning of domestication, and the end of domestication signals the beginning of romance. Romance is the engagement of individuals as representations of reality, allowing the dynamic to be offset and leading back to wholesome selfhood. However, this process cannot continue indefinitely, for the couple will eventually divert from the universal experience of their personhood and instead begin a domestic endeavor. This transition does not allow for offsetting within the relationship itself because domestication lacks the capacity to direct individuals "out there." It does not provide a nuanced perception of what exists beyond it. Instead, it offers a randomized encapsulation of reality that does not directly reflect individual happenstance, encapsulating an experience disconnected from time and space.

Thus, domestication cannot provide direction beyond itself, as it exists in an unmeasured plane of existence. Only the loss of domestication can initiate the journey toward reality, and domestication itself should —and cannot —be part of that initiation process.

The Central Locale and Universal Interaction

To refer to our original cause, the central locale requires only the cosmic elements for its necessary reaction and interaction. Beyond noting these two core themes—first, its universal element, and second, a counterpoise of its initial credence—there is also the necessity of social agreement.

For the centric locale, it must emulate nature in its perfected form, incorporating both its inclusive diversity and its distinguishing aspects. This means that without social agreement— continued contextual interest, the environment of the central locale would dwindle, leading to dependence on another locale that would assume its mantle. To remain a central locale, the process must ensure that the context of interaction remains proportionate to nature itself and its universal sentiment.

There can be cosmic elements that are not in agreement but still remain interactive due to their prevalence and evidential nature. When deviation occurs, requiring academic evidence—such as proving the existence of the sun, despite its obviousness—the interaction becomes conditional. The sun does not require proof for universal agreement; therefore, only instances requiring such validation become interactive material. A common theme in the central locale is the emergence of deviations that necessitate evidential research, postulating themselves as universal interactions while still requiring proof that excludes a portion of sociality. Those who either do not follow the evidence or do not agree with it automatically become the cause of dispersion, breaking the elemental interaction of the central locale.

Even if only a small portion of sociality is needed to validate the universal element as true and genuine, this is enough to cause it to lack the diversity necessary for being an interactive element of the central locale. We are beginning to see that the issue is not merely about evidence but about universal agreement, while still being reliant on nature as the subject. There could be a political or social agreement across the board without deviation or contestation, yet it would still fail to attain prominence as an interactive element for the central locale because it is not truly mirrored in nature.

Similarly, natural elements that affect only portions of sociality—such as poverty or disease—would not constitute a contextual interaction because they do not include the entire social body, despite their prevalence in nature. Furthermore, these are not direct products of nature itself but rather biological necessities that exist within nature. Weather patterns, for instance, are not biological necessities, yet they interact with biological life. Because they are not bound by necessity but still act as prevalent markers of interaction, they remain integral to social agreement. A social body may choose to disregard weather patterns, but since their effects are universal, even in negligence, they remain a factor.

For example, we might argue that the moon's prevalence does not directly affect individual circumstances on Earth and therefore should not be considered an interactive criterion. However, because there is widespread agreement that it is a celestial presence and a predominant natural element—coupled with its demonstrable effects on social structures, such as calendars—it qualifies as an effective interactive element. In contrast, an alignment of Jupiter and Saturn, despite being a celestial event, does not have a considerable dynamic permeation across social bodies and thus cannot be considered a predominant effect. There must be a direct effect, even if inconsequential, so that its further permeation through social bodies becomes considerable. The moon, for example, affects Earth biologically, yet it is primarily recognized through its luminescence. Its continual social permeation, especially through its role in structuring time, elevates it to the status of a universal element.

When a natural event is not initially a biological interaction but requires evidence at the outset of its interaction, even if social bodies later permeate its relevance, it remains a political rather than a universal interaction. If nature undergoes a change, its direct impact can serve as a prevalent interaction. For instance, if glaciers are melting, the experience of those living within that habitat provides a universal interaction based on the melting itself. However, if this phenomenon is framed within a doctrine, theory, or framework that contextualizes it as part of a broader interpretation of nature, then it ceases to be a universal interaction and instead becomes a political endeavor.

The change of seasons, for example, directly affects individuals, whether they notice it or not, and is permeable through sociality. If a society disregards weather, their ability to mitigate or adapt to its conditions would lead them to lose social interaction with it. However, weather still exerts a universal effect on individuals, meaning that divergence from it does not eliminate its conditions, as individuals remain dependent on weather circumstances. Even if an optimal construction shields individuals from weather conditions, they are still dependent on that construction, which in turn is dependent on weather. At some level, there is always a direct linkage between individuals and natural events, even when mediated through other conditions.

Two Lineages of Consciousness

Memory traces can follow two distinct paths: localized consciousness or universal consciousness. Localized consciousness serves as a reliable, viable, and immediate form of awareness, closely tied to one's immediate experiences. However, its limitation lies in the fact that it captures only a fraction of the universal lineage of consciousness, offering merely a semblance or encapsulation of the greater whole.

Universal consciousness, on the other hand, retains the full spectrum of dominant and predominant consciousness, allowing it to permeate the psyche in its entirety. Its drawback is that, while it encompasses the full scope of consciousness, it lacks the ability to continuously participate in everyday interaction. Due to its vastness, universal consciousness cannot be frequently recalled or repeated; rendering it a distant and elusive entity until it fully completes its permeation.

Technically, one could attempt to retain only the lineage of universal consciousness by continuously interacting with memory traces—recording every experience in high detail so that the permeation remains uninterrupted. However, because universal consciousness exists at a structural distance, it naturally retracts itself from immediate experience. To counteract this, one must establish traction and a structural framework to maintain the vitality of these memory traces. When this framework is lacking, the memory traces become distorted and degenerate. Instead of receiving consciousness in its pure form, one ends up conjuring mere projections of it. The structural distance then creates a disparity, severing the physical lineage between oneself and the universal experience.

Localized and Universal Consciousness

Localized consciousness is defined by its inability to supersede universal consciousness. It is not an attempt to be localized; rather, it lacks the ability, retainment, or necessity to overcome the permeation and predominant effect of the lineage of universal consciousness. This necessity arises because localized consciousness provides a real-time attachment to the structural system that extends into the universal realm. Additionally, it supplies conceptual data experienced in the present incarnation, allowing for an interaction with the universal consciousness experience. With a fully experienced encapsulation of universal consciousness, one can both engage at a local level and recognize universal consciousness as a viable, real-time system.

We must be clear: localized consciousness is not a version of domestication. It is an experience of true consciousness, only subservient to a memory trace of a surpassing lineage of consciousness. Domestication is the framework from which we determine the criteria distinguishing localized consciousness from universal consciousness. It is labeled "localized" simply because it does not meet the criterion of universal permeation. If an attempt is made to elevate localized consciousness to the universal level—thus superseding its lineage and disrupting the necessary permeation from prior universal consciousness—we experience a break in the flow.

On one side, we have a constellation of universal consciousness that has not yet permeated the psyche. On the other, a localized experience of consciousness may attempt to supersede universal consciousness. In such a case, the individual psyche ceases to function as a receptacle for continuous conscious flow. Instead, an enlarged localized consciousness, exceeding its proper bounds, comes into conflict with the necessary permeation of prior universal consciousness.

Even in the presence of a central or any specific locale, both lineages will be followed simultaneously. In a typical case, consciousness permeates a localized experience derived from a greater ordeal based on its past. Rather than perceiving each day as a novel emergence of consciousness, localized consciousness retracts upon itself, following a encapsulation of prior experience—one that serves as the helm of consciousness. The exposed moment does not sustain itself but fades into routine, with that routine drawing its vitality from the helm of consciousness. However, each moment differs, following a distinct vantage point of encapsulated consciousness. Today, it follows one aspect of consciousness exposure; tomorrow, another point of conjecture. In this way, consciousness exposure continues through the secondary junctions of experience.

The purpose of a secondary juncture is that there is no need to presume that an exposed experience of consciousness must be re-experienced. Rather, because such exposure cannot be fully actualized in real-time due to its material constraints, it becomes a continuing phenomenon. Portions of its material are distributed over time, allowing for the experience that was initially missed due to temporal limitations and the density of the material.

The moment of exposure is usually preceded by the culmination of these secondary junctures, which serve to fulfill the overall depth of the prior exposure. At the point where a void emerges, there arises a need for localized consciousness to transition into another exposure—one that will serve as the new helm moving forward.

Corporeal and Conceptual Consciousness

We have evolved to define *structural consciousness* and *conceptual consciousness* using a different metric system. Rather than proposing that the structure itself represents the concreteness of reality, we are more inclined to consider the process of the psyche in that regard. We operate under the presumption that the structure is the emanating factor, while the psyche's reception is secondary. We introduce the term corporeal consciousness to define the structure by its most authentic endeavor—representing the corporeal system in its entirety. In doing so, it avoids being reduced to merely one concrete aspect of the system, for it embodies the entire corporeal system rather than just its primary element.

Conversely, *conceptual consciousness* serves as the primary element of the corporeal system, acting as the mechanism upon which the corporeal system operates. This is to be considered authentic consciousness because it provides a direct interpretation of consciousness, whereas corporeal consciousness encompasses *conceptual consciousness* within a broader system. However, corporeal consciousness does not emanate consciousness directly—just as the body does not independently display mental configurations but operates as part of a system. One might advocate for the primacy of corporeal consciousness until they grasp a fundamental truth: all consciousness is a representation, and the biological system is not inherent to consciousness but rather a reflection of it.

Corporeal Representation in Consciousness

As much as corporeal representation aspires to be the composite picture of the corporeal system, it remains merely a representation of that system within the consciousness continuum. The biological system itself does not possess the opportunity or ability to serve as a representation. In a sense, corporeal consciousness functions as a simulative system—providing a reflection point that encompasses the entire system rather than just the continuum of consciousness. Without corporeal consciousness, one would be lost in the consciousness continuum, lacking an integrated view of the corporeal whole—even if that whole is only possible because of consciousness.

Thus, it is at the expense of *conceptual consciousness* that corporeal consciousness takes over, enabling the experience of composite consciousness (both in its authentic state and embodied structure), which includes both the corporeal system and its consciousness encapsulation.

Whenever we experience corporeal consciousness, we do not have authentic consciousness, and whenever we experience *conceptual consciousness*, we do not perceive the corporeal aspect of that consciousness. It is as if corporeal consciousness is the body and *conceptual consciousness* is the mind, with the entire process serving merely as the representation of the biological system. Corporeal consciousness relieves one from the erratic experience of authenticity, integrating the corporeal system against the unpredictable currents of a conceptual process.

Between Conceptual and Corporeal Consciousness

Corporeal consciousness does not permit the consciousness continuum to remain fixed in its locale so that the composite experience can take effect. Yet, it would be no match for the pure emanation of consciousness. Often, *conceptual consciousness* overtakes a corporeal domain simply because there is no effective separation. When faced with the choice either to participate in authentic consciousness or to contain it within the corporeal structure, the result is invariably authentic consciousness.

We observe the proximity and dependency of corporeal consciousness through the lens of *conceptual consciousness* because the latter is

Corporeal and Conceptual Consciousness

fundamental to the organization as a whole—since corporeal consciousness is also engineered as a consciousness process. Although corporeal consciousness appears as a simplistic biological system in its representation (contrasting with raw consciousness), we have assumed that position by referring to it as *structural consciousness*. Yet, it is not the structure in a concrete state but rather another facet of the consciousness system—one that seeks to represent the entire corporeal experience rather than merely the continuum of *conceptual consciousness*.

For this reason, we cannot establish a center of consciousness without incorporating both corporeal and *conceptual consciousness*. Corporeal representation offsets and houses *conceptual consciousness*, which—without such integration—would become erratic manifestations of consciousness, lost within the corporeal system and misaligned with its structure.

Balancing Consciousness: The Need for Integration

As the encapsulation of consciousness increases, so too does the need for corporeal consciousness to balance it. A corporeal consciousness lacking the sophistication to accommodate a higher level of consciousness will eventually inhibit the ongoing expansion of consciousness in the psyche. Without sufficient corporeal representation to contain that consciousness, it cannot integrate into the system.

Likewise, and with even greater consequence, corporeal consciousness—without sufficient inclusion of *conceptual consciousness*—becomes lost within the system. Since its primary function is to provide a composite picture of corporeal representation for a given encapsulation of consciousness, when it is unable to do so, it recedes into the background, losing its justification for effective formation.

We do find that the major impression of consciousness does indeed emanate from structural or corporeal consciousness, even though it is merely the representation of the entire system, which contains only a limited encapsulation of consciousness. This is because it most accurately mirrors the biological system—and what captures one's attention more than the validation of selfhood?

For this reason, one may believe they have made significant strides in consciousness, sensing a stronger validation of their physical form, which seems illuminating. Analogous to the sentimental feeling a holiday evokes, which can give rise to the assumption that it is the center of vitality. However, without the inclusion of *conceptual consciousness*, this experience loses its psychological impact on the overall outcome of their consciousness.

They may acquire a greater reception, but when that reception is not filled appropriately, it becomes superfluous and retreats into the background. If one were to follow the psychological experience of the initial validation, they would notice that the truly illuminating aspect is not the corporeal representation but rather the encapsulation of consciousness it contains.

After accepting the mistaken assumption that it is simply a larger corporeal representation, one loses connection with the initial experience and its accompanying encapsulation of consciousness. In this state, they become the entire corporeal ordeal, yet they no longer know how to access the encapsulation of consciousness contained within it. Over time, corporeal consciousness will cease to be experienced as an encapsulation of consciousness because the effect of its reception has taken precedence.

Conceptual consciousness, on the other hand, without a reception with corporeal representation, either for the individual becomes erratic in the social sphere, or for the locality or group, becomes distinctly separated from larger localities and groups. Another problematic issue is that *conceptual consciousness*, which is often experienced alongside corporeal consciousness, becomes lost from its center and continuum. The center is lost because consciousness is, after all, a reflection of a biological state, with the corporeal representation serving as the mediator. When there is a detachment, consciousness does not relate or participate as if it were part of a distinctive system of affairs.

Second to this is the lack of continuum. Consciousness, as a conceptual marker, is a conversation to some degree—one that must continue in a dynamic fashion. Without a clear continuum—one that reaches back into history and stretches outward to the future—that incarnation of consciousness would lack any social relevance. The primary method to maintain continuity for consciousness is through the offset of corporeal representation, which acts as a mediator between erratic consciousness and the strict necessity of consciousness. The corporeal representation, understanding a specific encapsulation of consciousness, can act and take notice of a lack of consistency in that specific material. What will not be noticed during the experience of genuine consciousness becomes apparent when observed within the corporeal representation. Immediately, a vulnerability or overstretched notion can become clear because the entire system is available for observation.

However, as noted, the corporeal representation does not take into account all of consciousness but only specific strands, so it may be correct in its presumptions, only to be proven wrong when all things are considered. The corporeal representation may notice a biological discrepancy—in which there is a lack of attention to biological reality—but cannot discern more than that. When we consider that even the biological system offsets its internal workings to give precedence to other parts, we gain a fuller picture. According to the level of consciousness the corporeal system is tasked with, there will be a consideration of a more elaborate understanding of the corporeal system.

We can find simplistic corporeal systems function with minimal consciousness, overlooking vast aspects of experience. Such systems possess just enough awareness to initiate inquiry but lack the full experience of consciousness. This is evident across levels of consciousness. A primal human, for example, may rely on a restricted range of consciousness to maintain stability, using limited knowledge within a narrow framework. For such an individual, venturing into unknown domains is daunting, as the risks seem to outweigh the rewards. Conversely, within more evolved forms of consciousness, this concern diminishes—not because differentiation requires rational justification, but because, at such levels, the corporeal representation no longer perceives it as a necessary limitation.

Corporeal representation only acknowledges the consciousness it encapsulates, forming conclusions based solely on that encapsulation. Within its scope, it often regards its understanding as comprehensive. Yet, contradictions arise when multiple encapsulations of consciousness exist within the same corporeal framework. At any moment, a corporeal representation encapsulates a segment of consciousness while also inheriting the constraints of previous structures. This lineage shapes its framework, embedding subtle references to historical consciousness within the corporeal system. The advancement of a corporeal system lies in its ability to integrate this historical consciousness while navigating the present.

An individual participating in such a structure may sense the expansion of its corporeal framework but may fail to recognize the complexity of its historical integration. What is immediately apparent is the appeal of the expanded corporeal representation, particularly in its present reception of consciousness. This can be demonstrated anecdotally: when societal reflection is absent, the skeletal nature of these structures becomes evident. It is not the social participation itself that sustains these systems, but the *conceptual consciousness* they hold, which is then received within that locality. The prior consciousness is not inherently embedded in the system; rather, it remains dormant within the corporeal framework until activated.

Consciousness, Memory, and Systemic Integration

Details and structural elements are embedded within a system much like layers of an artwork, whose meaning is not merely found in the final composition but in each preceding layer. The current encapsulation of consciousness, absorbed into this complex corporeal structure, has the potential to retrace earlier forms of consciousness through systemic reception. Thus, even if the present consciousness follows a particular theme, because consciousness itself transcends any singular encapsulation, the entire corporeal structure becomes illuminated, revealing past iterations of consciousness.

We see this effect in historical centers: when contemporary consciousness engages with them, it does not create new meaning but instead highlights prior precedents. A discernible gap emerges between the corporeal system's historical record and the present consciousness. This system functions because consciousness retains a memory of its preceding forms. While it prioritizes its current state, it inevitably casts light on the historical corporeal representation.

However, as noted in other works, it is easy to become absorbed in this historical consciousness, losing engagement with the present. When consciousness is structured within a memory framework to reactivate a past state, corporeal representation merely delivers that encapsulation of consciousness—it cannot restore the broader development of consciousness itself. This suggests that

We agree with this premise in any skill: the restructuring and maintenance of that skill will only be considered if it is based on a distinct experience that demands such a state. When a skill goes under maintenance without a pressing demand—say, when a doctor steps away from practice to reduce the anatomical structure—they do so without activating consciousness. When they return to practice, they will still function within the prior doctor's state. Only during that period can they retrieve new education according to the demands of the practice. The educated elements that do not serve that demand will cease to be a participant in the practicing solution.

If a corporeal system restructures itself to follow parameters that seem to fit the dissemination of consciousness, without activating that consciousness, those elements will cease to exist when consciousness is activated. The restructuring process did not entail the demand for consciousness in its reception and was done on an individual level. This means that when consciousness appears in the picture, it will not reach those restructuring elements. It could be the case that if the restructuring elements prove to be an antidote to the current encapsulation of consciousness, they will be included retroactively, a general process of education.

This is why any political or group attempt to restructure a locality to become a habitat for more consciousness—or at least the appearance of it—would be futile. Each layer of that structure was not enabled by a consciousness experience, so any new encapsulation of consciousness will not reach all parts of that structured system. Only when each structural or corporeal representation change is based on defining consciousness substance does the reception take effect. Even after the encapsulation of consciousness fades away, its residual memory is maintained within the corporeal structure. It will be immediately activated when new encapsulated abridgments of consciousness arise, despite changes in that consciousness.

Thus, a city structure built competently should be activated with any new consciousness, starting from its earliest recorded experience of consciousness instilled into its corporeal structure. This is why expanding empires grow exponentially: because with each new encapsulation of consciousness, it permeates all the earlier corporeal representations. This is also why they become more vulnerable with expansion: without innovative encapsulations of consciousness, the entire system and its subsidiaries collapse.

The definition of a nuanced continuation of consciousness depends on the concurrent dynamic of the prior instance. Without the data code of the previous consciousness case, there is no ability for continuation, and it will merely revert to the earliest memory. Thus, we have a perpetual process where the nuanced gain of consciousness fades into memory, and an earlier recorded consciousness gain takes precedence, continuing from that standpoint. However, because it is a memory—something already enlightened but recreated—it delineates the entire process. Instead of being an infusion of working consciousness substance, it becomes a recreation of consciousness as if it were nuanced.

This is why a consciousness system takes on a sense of repeating itself: sometimes, it simply repeats itself. The corporeal representation that receives the encapsulation of consciousness based on the retrieval of an earlier state loses potency—similar to the second or third meeting of a social counterpart, which might represent a deeper experience of interpersonal relationships but does not compare to the initial exposure. Therefore, a retrieval of consciousness lacks the ability to follow through the entire corporeal system, especially in reviving its earlier periods.

The memory of the first exposure—that of the initial enlightenment—remains intact, while the later memory serves as an exposure interacting with subparts of the initial reaction. When we input or re-input a memory into a consciousness infrastructure, we are not attempting to continue the conversation and dynamic exchange of the consciousness encapsulation, but instead intending to provide a memory of an earlier exposure. The reason we can do this is that the initial exposure has an imprint strong enough to fortify it into the concrete framework, allowing us to act on the memory—or encapsulation of the earlier consciousness frame—and initiate an interaction with this domain.

The Stagnation of Memory-Based Relationships and Consciousness

When you realize a memory framework to initiate a prior state of consciousness, the corporeal representation will only be effective in providing that encapsulation of consciousness and becomes lost in its ability to revitalize earlier aspects of consciousness attainment. It is almost as if the process must work on a skeletal basis, where the corporeal representation is only able to house this specific consciousness, remaining in the background in its entire process and growth in earlier frames. By using an earlier frame, we do not have the ability to revitalize another, especially one that precedes the initial exposure that this memory serves.

I liken this phenomenon to a relationship in which regular interaction relies on the memory traces of prior events. During the interval of reliance on memory, however, the relationship cannot refile or realign its already concentrated elements.

While the relationship represents a long lineage of developmental stages —where consciousness has permeated and sustained its foundation—if it relies solely on the memory trace of a specific exposed event, it will not be able to fully permeate its foundational space. Even though the foundation remains intact and the relationship may appear sophisticated, it is still a dormant element that lacks the ability to sustain or provide a true experiential presence. Only when the relationship undergoes fresh moments of exposure can it access and activate those foundational elements.

This is why a relationship can endure for a considerable period without active engagement, relying on a prior exposure defense that continuously retracts in search of additional memory traces. Yet it does not fully integrate its foundational elements because it is not an encapsulation of consciousness but merely a memory trace of it.

For this reason, stagnation becomes a continuous phenomenon as long as there is no activation for new exposure. The entire relationship, therefore, depends on a receding memory that prevents new consciousness from engaging its foundational structure. Because activation of the foundation is necessary, the foundational elements gradually begin to lose their stability and defining criteria within the system.

Without the input of newly encapsulated consciousness, the corporeal representation—encompassing the preceding stages of development—cannot maintain its integrity within the system. Although these foundational elements may still be present in the background, even as memory, they emit only a limited functional influence on earlier stages, insufficient to provide the viability needed for continued progression.

At some point, with prolonged reliance on memory elements of the foundational footprint, traction is lost. The system then becomes increasingly dependent on approaching the continuum of consciousness without a corporeal representation. Without the presence of current consciousness and its memory traces, nothing remains—not even a retraction of memory.

It is as if the reserves of memory become depleted in an attempt to sustain some semblance of consciousness, and when those reserves dry up, all that remains is the present, fleeting experience of consciousness. At that moment, any loss of exposure to current consciousness—which itself depends on a receding memory—results in an inability to retain further memory traces.

Even if one attains an enlightenment of consciousness—a provision of exposure that leads the chorus of the entire system—this exposure will not be in alignment with the foundational footprint. It is as if one finds the right direction to continue consciousness but without any prior material as a basis. One may stretch further in the pursuit of enlightenment, but without

The Structure of Consciousness

a prior database of foundational elements, those aspects will not be infused with a continuing semblance or the power to disseminate consciousness.

Whether for the individual —where the psyche may continue onward with this consciousness encapsulation at the helm—or for a locality, the system lacks dissemination power because prior exposure to consciousness was not retained. One might follow certain parameters to gain access to the helm of consciousness but will not have the ability to disseminate that information, as it was never an entailment of one's own localization that reached toward that consciousness.

In a sense, this is the natural order of affairs—where one must reach toward the helm of consciousness without necessarily having developed toward it. Taken to the extreme, however, it results in a lack of substance capable of disseminating consciousness beyond the immediate experience itself.

The same applies to a locality, where consciousness exposed at a given moment lacks the ability to disseminate further because it does not regard —or is incapable of regarding—its prior foundational elements. This occurs precisely because the consciousness is exposed at the point of dynamical exchange rather than through a continuous dynamical process. The very fact that it does not follow the dynamical process may allow for further enlightenment, yet only when we adhere to such a process do we realize how much attention is required at various exchange points—so much so that further progression toward enlightenment is rarely entertained.

Consciousness, Social Exchange, and the Continuum

On the one hand, there is the approach of interacting with the consciousness continuum, on the other, the method of appropriating oneself as part of its sequence. These two approaches employ differing methods. To interact with consciousness does not necessitate a specific social exchange—at least, not an agreed-upon one. Rather, it depends on whether the exchange is socially recognized and actualized. The key point is the interaction itself, concluded one enters into communion with the continuum, regardless of how this is facilitated.

Of course, an individual remains bound to their identity, and therefore, when engaging in the interaction, it inevitably reflects the social sequence. However, this does not mean they must conform to a predetermined position within the realized social exchange. Instead, they mirror the social exchange solely to facilitate interaction with consciousness. The nature of this mirroring is determined by the individual's developed social state.

By contrast, the process of appropriating oneself as a position within the consciousness system is inherently tied to environmental surroundings. This is not due to external limitations but rather because the individual treats social exchange as the principal means of succession within the consciousness sequence. In truth, this assumption is flawed. Social exchange is merely a construct—a system of rulings and parameters designed to aid in the understanding and guidance of interaction with consciousness. It is not, however, the fundamental gateway to consciousness. Was this the case, there would be a singular, universal social system. Yet, in reality, countless social systems exist, each functioning as an appropriation of the consciousness sequence.

Furthermore, when a social system evolves beyond simply representing its constituents and instead becomes a consciousness continuum with distinct interactivity, it transitions into a corporeal system. Such a system does not entail direct interaction with consciousness itself, nonetheless moderately with its embryonic form, housed within an interactive structure. This encapsulation of consciousness is limited—it is present in neither real-time nor expansive within the sequence. Instead, it serves as a mere framework through which interaction is approached.

One can, however, interact with consciousness independently of the corporeal system or, in this context, without social exchange. This affords the advantage of engaging with the entire sequence in real-time. The caveat, however, is that the individual remains shaped by their own developmental stage of social systems and interactivity. As a result, their interaction with consciousness will always be mediated by the internal social structure, such that has been cultivated. Even if they transcend the necessity of social exchange within their perceptual system, they remain bound to the movement of their internal social framework.

An individual is fundamentally a creation of their social environment, and the internalized aspect of that sociality serves as the point of entry into any interaction they choose to engage in. When one's internal social exchange is well developed, their interaction—regardless of the context—will align with that social spectrum. Conversely, if their internal social exchange is underdeveloped, their interaction with consciousness will be limited to the equivalent of their social capacity. Whether the social exchange is internal or external, the two will mirror one another, forming the foundation for interaction.

In other words, if an individual remains reliant on an internal social system that has not been revisited or evolved beyond its initial formation—such as a relationship frozen in its premature stage—the lack of development results in an unchanging projection of that relationship. The inability to progress beyond this state means that all subsequent interactions with consciousness will be constrained by the original social framework.

This creates the illusion of a continuous, unbroken relationship, as if one were trapped in an endless loop of its preliminary manifestations. Every new interaction will be shaped by this static vantage point. In the context of consciousness, this relationship is projected outward, such that any engagement with consciousness is filtered through the linear constraints of that original social position.

It is as if the individual embodies a fixed point on the spectrum of the continuum. More precisely, the relationship itself becomes the total framework within which interaction occurs, even when it appears to be an external engagement. What seems like an external interaction is, in reality, the extension of an internal dynamic—one that has not been further developed. This undeveloped internal interaction is thus projected onto the external world, shaping the entirety of one's engagement with consciousness and defining its boundaries.

Dependencies, Growth, and Evolutionary Interactions

When the consciousness system is running properly, dependencies are reduced, and constituents are rewarded without the need for individual effort. Whatever the movements may be—whether developed in proper formation or deficient for a consciousness system—the individual becomes a habitat of growth because the system's permeation flows downstream. One may mistakenly attribute development to personal effort because the system is so balanced that any choice naturally leads to proper inclusion.

The reason is that the environment plays such a consequential role that individual parameters become almost secondary. Specific choices appear somewhat inconsequential in fostering growth. For instance, an individual raised in a particular socio-economic background can often be predicted to follow a certain trajectory. Despite their individual attributes, with a competent environment at a particular level, individuality plays only a secondary role. Individuality becomes a primary factor only when the environment lacks the necessary support, forcing each personal choice to navigate between the lesser of two problematic solutions.

In a properly functioning consciousness system, individual choices merely enhance development, ensuring that everyone receives a sufficient and often satiating portion of vitality. Dependencies diminish because external systems require little to integrate into the system's permeation, enabling autonomy in their own right. This might seem paradoxical: when individuality is less necessary, there is more autonomy, while when individuality is fundamental to vitality, there is less autonomy.

It is similar to functional parental figures—an adult child raised in a well-supported environment does not rely on their parents for autonomy because even a minimal encapsulation of influence is sufficient to sustain them. However, this semblance of autonomy is not true autonomy. The adult who gains independence through simplistic retention of their parental figures' influence is not autonomous in the sense of individual force but rather in the sense of lacking direct dependency. They are, in fact, embodiments of their parental figures with little deviation.

Similarly, in a proper consciousness system, individuals and non-central entities attain autonomy through minimal doses of support. However, they do not act as independent entities but as complete embodiments of the system, eliminating the need for individual deviation. In some sense, this already signals decline—an assumption of autonomy when, in reality, there is no individuality. They merely follow the system's wavelengths without guardrails. Furthermore, the lack of individuality results in vitality without a nuanced personal foundation, making them mere actors rather than embodiments of the permeation. The reason this appears as autonomy is the absence of disparity in their movements—precisely that they lack individuality, acting only as extensions of the system without nuance. The eventual decline is inevitable. If all individuals adopt this natural approach, the system will stagnate, lacking individual agency to drive innovation and nuance. True autonomy, in the sense of individuality, is only burdensome in two cases:

1. When an individual, despite the system's inherent goodness, insists on participating from a personal vantage point—choosing the risk of change and separation from the system's pervasive consciousness. This is a costly

Dependencies, Growth, and Evolutionary Interactions

endeavor, as mediating between an individual consciousness and the structural system is complex and filled with existential dread.

2. When systemic degeneration forces individuals into such a state, leaving no choice but to perform this separation without any resolution, as the system fails to complete their personhood.

In a properly functioning consciousness system, individuals receive enough permeation to sustain their direction, ensuring that even minimal exposure suffices for their vitality. The ideal system resembles a perfected energy source—balanced at its inception, requiring no additional effort beyond the individual's choice to engage with it for nuanced vitality. Its transmission code is transparent, requiring no reinterpretation, and adaptable to different stages of individual development.

A perfected system is tangible across social and age spectrums, akin to a well-crafted educational material that is inclusive to all ages, such as Shakespeare or the Bible. Competent infrastructure serves all ages—the adult for nuance and the child for relevance. Infrastructure is an essential component of the consciousness system because, by definition, it must serve the full spectrum rather than a particular demographic. If it catered only to a specific group, it would cease to be infrastructure and instead become a private dwelling. One defining factor of infrastructure is its service to the 'public,' whereas private dwellings cater to specific demographics. Similarly, a competent consciousness system serves the entire spectrum rather than a select group, sometimes giving the false impression of being simplistic or underdeveloped. However, any material that does not meet the full spectrum's needs will be lost to social evolution because it does not integrate with the full chain of human development.

This notion of a continuous evolutionary chain is what distinguishes a proper consciousness system. When it fails to encompass the full spectrum, individuals cannot fully assimilate its material due to a biological buffer that creates disparity. This disparity between evolutionary reality and the consciousness material forces individuals into a dilemma: they must choose between their biological reality and the consciousness system. Either choice results in loss—prioritizing biological direction detaches them from their role in the system, while prioritizing the system detaches them from individuality.

As a result, the individual must become a private consciousness system, embodying the complete framework to navigate external interactions effectively. They must understand the consciousness system's parameters to make consistently sound choices, and each deviation carries a greater impact because the mere act of choice represents a renunciation of a certain realm.

Cosmic Influences and Political Systems

The centric locale has a major strain in procuring a *contextual interactive embodiment*. There will be intervals where it reduces into an interactive space, where, if one were to bring their own context, they would engage in a circumvented personal embodiment, due to the interactivity of that domicile.

The act of fashioning a centric locale toward expansion creates such an absence of contextual direction to its degeneration. The locale depends on a universal system, dismissing anything non-universal from its sociality. This leaves only two possibilities of remediation: one of political nature and the other of cosmic nature—both antitheses' to the centric locale, as *nature* is above its predisposition and politics is beneath it.

The downside of a universal system is its inability to procure contextual direction, which is essential for an *interactive embodied environment*. Therefore, the elements that can provide this—whether natural or political—become the liminal space of social direction. It is no coincidence that the centric locale relies on these two, despite its prominence among them. The reality of nature must establish a sequential pattern of connection, allowing for the effect of expansion. Expansion requires structural attachment—adherence to a system and process that remains connected despite differentiation and complexity.

When cosmic interference occurs, whether slight or major, it disrupts the notion of sequential patterning. Even though infrastructure claims to be sequential, the cosmic reality is not. However, such disruptions are only understood as such because of the belief that interference is a structural existence. For example, rain is seen as a separating factor within a sequential infrastructure, even though rain itself does not inherently differentiate land. Because the experience of rain creates a sentiment of differentiation—especially in its realized individual interactions—it disrupts belief in sequential patterning. Yet, a society can bypass this experience by recognizing that cosmic change does not preclude sequential differentiation but rather introduces uniqueness within it.

In fact, even major cosmic events—such as hurricanes, tornadoes, and viruses—can be seen as mere uniqueness of the cosmic reality, to which the sequential system is not differentiated. But because there is realized

Dependencies, Growth, and Evolutionary Interactions

personal interference, in which the experienced reality of that cosmic interference is of a certain degree, one must confer with the senses to understand that the experienced differentiation is not a genuine marker of nature, but rather its nuanced character.

Moreover, one notices that the sequential pattern of the infrastructure of the centric locale engages in a constrained activity: to disrupt individuals so that the system continues in proper sequential pattern. These expenses occur regularly and throughout the system, ranging from social self-consciousness to the loss of life—, which mirrors cosmic interference in a similar pattern. We could even demonstrate through statistical analysis that the range of incidentals aims for the infrastructure outweighs those of major cosmic events. The difference is that we experience cosmic events personally, while the incidental aspects of the system often go unnoticed by the individual or by society at large.

The Political System and the Centric Locale

Internal Dynamics

The centric locale is dependent on the political system in which it is geographically embedded—not as an agency subject to it, but as a consequence of being surrounded by it. If the political system fails to integrate with the centric locale, the locale itself does not suffer, since its dependency is geographical, not conceptual. To preserve its universality, the centric locale must distinguish itself from political embeddedness, avoiding political determinism in order to act in a universal capacity, untethered from any particular political structure.

This dependency is most apparent in the need for a minimal standard of boundary protection and the mitigation of external threats. Once this baseline is met, the locale becomes fairly autonomous. While a constitution is vital to the political system, for the centric locale consciousness and its cogitation process serve as its own self-generating "constitution." The formal constitution of the political body holds no authority over the centric locale's cogitation, though it may be referenced due to shared characteristics.

The entire construction of the political body is the emulation and provision of the centric locale as a provision of security and stability. For example, if one observes a profound individual who lacks protection precisely because they must preserve their profundity, others may impose an external form of protection to meet their needs—despite the fact that the individual never requested or sought such provision. This is how a political body ascends from society: in the notice of a sequential centric locale, it raises a standard that mirrors such a reality, in order that it can do the necessary deeds, such that can only be done as an external process.

They are not an ascendancy due to society but a sociality willing to reside outside the centric locale and provide the provision in order that they are maintained, especially for those elements that cannot be done by the internal system. The primary necessity to which a centric locale cannot arrange based on its self-generating terms is physical protection. It constitutes an exchange system that neither asserts its autonomy nor becomes conspicuous at any point in time. This becomes the chief concern of the political body—to provide what is most essential but cannot be addressed within the internal framework of that cogitation.

Entry Points and the Limits of Regulation

The consciousness system does include itself into individuality and provide regulation and control; however, it cannot take a stake in the general influx between itself and what is external from it, for it comprises whoever participates. The participant can be of a disposition that will disrupt the system, requiring an external body to oversee that flow. This also includes the notion of more diversity and conversion in its populating masses, for that may be the provision for which it cannot express by virtue of its silence. This will be another entry point but is not the usual preoccupation of the political body and thus is not as available.

This would have them follow the recognition of population flow of the political body in accordance with cogitation to identify the various details that make up such an analysis. This is why it becomes the major point of conjecture for any *shadow* of an internal political system, in which they focus on the notion of ethnicity, identity, and other various factors that are necessary when the political body makes the decisions for the population flow for rumination.

Of course, the political body does not want to embellish upon this analysis, because it is work that dehumanizes and deconstructs social value for insurance of a system. The centric locale cannot even begin such a process because it is solely reliant upon individual procedures that do not have to do with their general makeup. However, in the analysis of population control, it does require a general recognition of the makeup so

The Political System and the Centric Locale

that it can provide the necessary provisions for the centric locale—whether it is the inclusion of more diversity, and to what is considered diverse for that locale, or to the regulation of certain inclusions, and to what is considered such. This is the dirty work of a political body, for it must do so without the appearance because it would affect the experience the exposure had it become known that it is population was controlled with such intention.

Another provision of the political body is to manage individuals or groups that engage the centric locale without genuine consciousness—becoming its "*shadow*." An entity cannot handle its own *shadow*, so the political body must ensure a minimum standard that prevents impairment of the locale's marginalized elements.

The workings of the political body are generally external functions that do not make themselves known to the centric locale. Because they are tasked with the most sensitive aspects of that locale—ensuring the elements that cannot be mitigated by the system itself—the political body becomes avoided as an entity in its entirety. The interactions with it are tasks that are not conferring a compulsory standard for continuance, or, it pertains to the various *shadows* of the system that attach themselves to the political body in relation to their connection with that localized system.

Thus, the most politically charged individuals or groups of a centric locale can always be identified as the *shadow* of the system. Without the ability to interact directly with consciousness, they rely on the political body as a medium. Extended to the entire state, those deeply involved in politics often those who have not accessed the process of emanation and, therefore, rely on the political body to mediate that engagement. However, this interaction is primarily grounded in the political body's role in regulating them, ensuring that their actions do not disrupt the underlying infrastructure or its process of propagation. As such, the nature of this relationship is one of regulation rather than genuine engagement. This dynamic reveals to the constituents that they are, in essence, the *shadow* of the system—defined and constrained by this very relationship. The political body will address their concerns only when it serves to protect the centric process; it is not structured to attend to their needs.

Upon the perspective of these constituents, it is the only possibility of gaining any provision of consciousness, by adhering to the political body, which does have a relationship with the centric locale and its propagation. However, that is not the purpose of this relationship, for they are not nearby to spread the exposure but rather to protect it. Expenditure of the political body to gain entry, is attempting to utilize a system that does not have such as its objective. It is true that one gains an iota of exposure through the political, but that lens is not overlooking the cogitation itself but rather its aspects that prerequisite mitigation. We cannot determine the consequence of propagation from a political body but only the problematic aspects to which they are tasked.

If we examined the daily activity of political leadership, we would find most tasks are protective—physically and conceptually. These are the specific burdens to which centric locales cannot bear without foregoing its autonomy. Adhering to these political functions will not lead to an understanding of propagation; at best, one can observe how external entities respond to it and how the political body decides to intervene.

Consequently, those seeking access via political structures experience only external interpretation—often distorted by adversarial actors. Internal *shadow*s of consciousness depend on the state's external *shadow*s for access. They retain power by mediating entry, never followed for their own sake but for what their presence implies—what is missing or distorted.

Shadows and Misconceptions of Rumination

The aspect, which *shadow*s perceive, is the way external entities respond to the process of propagation, and the manner in which they choose to confront that reality. Thus, the only path to exposure lies in following the political body's protective engagement with those external entities that presume propagation—however it manifests—and respond accordingly. These responses are not necessarily grounded in the entities' structural foundations or their authentic perception of the experience.

As a result, for those who seek engagement with exposure through political bodies, the most problematic and externalized elements of the state—and their interpretations of such—become the gateway. Although there may be a genuine reflective experience for these external entities, their interpretations rarely undergo the necessary deconstruction to align with the irregular, often paradoxical nature of true exposure.

Consequently, the internal *shadow* of the rumination system becomes dependent on the external *shadow* of the state itself—this being the primary access point. But due to a strained relationship with these external actors, and especially because of their deep embodiment within the political system, they do not follow its emanation as it is, but rather be in competition with it, misled by a misinterpretation rooted in allegiance to the state. Thus, they become dependent on a distorted understanding of propagation, embracing its inverse—not out of clarity, but out of loyalty.

Decline, Stagnation, and Identity Disintegration

The experience of structuring one's life as a *shadow* is deeply unwelcoming. (In other works, we will explore its purpose and significance more fully.) It is not so much a renunciation in the name of consciousness, but rather a quiet obscurity—an absence that could be filled by anyone or anything, without intention or meaning. More poignantly, these individuals are not reflecting; instead, they are perceived only in terms of what is missing, as if soundlessly posturing the question: *Why does their presence feel dim in contrast to what is luminous?*

They are thus observed through the most decaying aspects. Any notion of their own developed identity or deconstructed elements will be meticulously avoided. The further the inquiry moves away from their deconstructiveness, the more it detaches from constructed expansion. This would, in effect, promote those aspects of their being that would remain constrained.

Such an approach risks enlarging what is typically seen as a moral downgrade, making it the quintessential aspect of their identity—for that is what renders them a relevant conduit for expansion. It is precisely the promotion of these *shadow*-like aspects that entangles them in a process of generational decline, a descent that may never be retraced.

Even if such a state appears to offer a solution—existing without the expense elements of expansion, yet remaining within its realm with limited vitality—this position would inevitably degrade its moral stature. It is as if they are compelled to decline further into *shadow* rather than maintaining stagnation within a certain comfort of it. This is the natural reality of affairs: nothing remains stagnant, nor can anything merely posture as such. The question then arises—at what cost does this mode of alleviation come?

External Dynamics

The relationship between the centric locale and the political body is complex. The latter is tasked with ensuring the essential provisions necessary for the centric function, while the former provides the interactive details and material necessary to construct an accurate composite picture for the political body's understanding. Any deviation from these roles leads to the degeneration of both entities.

When the centric locale, which must have a certain representation, finds itself at odds with the political body, this can stem from two possibilities: either the political body is no longer aimed at protecting expansion, or the representatives misunderstand what is needed to sustain it.

A participant within the enlargement arrangement cannot independently determine the needs of the locale, as their perspective is shaped by their own position within the system. Their calculations are inevitably limited to their particular vantage point, which they might take to be the true pathway. Instead, an external body must oversee these necessities, precisely because it can observe the system without being bound by it.

However, it is possible that the political body lacks all the necessary information to form sincere conclusions. In such a case, representatives may argue that it is not entrenched enough in the material to accurately assess what is obligatory. Yet, if the material has already been integrated into the political body, only a single point of contention remains, the political body's deviation from its roots and foundational obligations. In such cases, its objectives have shifted away from recognizing the primacy of expansion itself.

Deviation of the Political Body

To understand a political body and its deviation, we must first recognize that if it loses its foundational structure, it cannot employ effectively as a system of protection and provision. A political body's essential nature is to protect and provide, and for this, it requires a structured system with a sequential pattern—a necessary component for any political engineering. Without such a sequential orientation, there is no reason for an overarching system of provision and protection. Protection would become localized, and provision would depend on its distinctions. Therefore, a political body must

The Political System and the Centric Locale

maintain a sequential relationship between its systems to ensure the benefits of protection and provision.

When a political body deviates, it may seek a novel locale that serves its need for sequential patterns of provision and protection. However, if it shifts to a locale that is not centrally oriented but follows a suboptimal sequential pattern, it has strayed from its political roots.

This raises the question of the periphery in respect to the central locale. In such cases, the political body must ignore its true stature to accommodate external needs. If a political body requires regulation of the population, it emphases its efforts on the masses. If the protection of external entities is needed, those individuals will be utilized for that purpose as well. Ultimately, all tasks necessary for the political action to be effective are carried out by these peripheral factions. The political body cannot rely on individuals involved in eminence, as the structure is meant to ensure the autonomy of the centric system. Using its members for provision would present a fundamental issue.

Thus, there is reciprocity between the political body and the peripheral locales. The locales gain access to propagation through political means—though often in the background—while the political body expenditures individuals and groups to support political actions necessary for the protection and provision of the centric system. The relationship between the political body and these peripheral factions resembles a unified system, existing at the periphery of the exposed system, to provide what is needed and what cannot be generated internally by the autonomous system. In this way, the political system operates as a renunciation of the centric system and its individuals, with external factions fulfilling those needs. This explains the prominence of the notion of a *public servant*: it symbolizes service to the centric system while remaining external to it.

From this, we see how easily a political body can deviate, shifting its concentration to the periphery. Since it already maintains an embedded relationship with these peripheral systems, it becomes natural for the political body to shift its function from protecting and providing solely for the centric system to doing so for the periphery.

Yet, we must also acknowledge that the periphery of the centric system still requires a degree of sequential pattern, even if it does not behold the same significance as the central system. This means that the peripheral systems must still be governed by the political body to maintain a necessary level of organization. The political body cannot just expense the periphery to serve its own ends; it must ensure that the periphery retains a functional

The Structure of Consciousness

structure to prevent it from fracturing into disjointed factions. In protecting the central system, the political body must also preserve the integrity of its periphery—because a dysfunctional periphery risks undermining the entire structure. Proper renunciation must occur before any true shedding of components can take place. Therefore, at times, the political body must care for the periphery to maintain oversight and prevent it from decaying into dysfunction.

Another essential aspect lies in the provisions supplied by the state's non-eminent factions. These groups, though differentiated from the core system, serve as reflective counterparts, offering external development that in turn influences the center. This development fosters private growth, which—though emerging outside the central structure—ultimately feeds back into it as an asset.

However, an asset only becomes valuable when it returns to its center. If expansion remains external, it vestiges as an unrealized gain. When the system operates properly—benefiting from various interrelated factors, the political body helps to integrate this external development into the central system, enriching its diversity and vitality. The centric system, being focused, depends on external input to supplement its narrow scope.

The political body, in its role, mediates this dynamic, ensuring the system functions smoothly. If the periphery of the political system lacks a structured format that provides it with some autonomy and resemblance to the central system, individuals will be unable to engage in meaningful personal development. Without such a structure, they would be enclosed in an infertile locale, devoid of the imaginative space necessary for growth. It is, therefore, a semblance of an eminent-like structure—not for security or actual exposure—but to allow for external development. This development can later re-enter the system, becoming a vital contribution.

This is why we find both the political body and the propagating system adhering to a population and infrastructure external to any real effect of propagating aspects: because of the possibility that individuals can serve as assets, eventually contributing to the internal system. It is almost as if a significant population is maintained for the meager return of complementary individuals who bring development based on that semblance—thus providing what the consciousness cognition cannot. People within the system can only develop according to its internal rules, which may lead to proficiency, but not necessarily innovation or change.

This structure extends beyond the state's boundaries, affecting all factions that receive propagating influences, regardless of their distance from the core. If external factions are developing in ways that contribute to the political system, they offer individual development that becomes a significant asset to the internal system. It is, therefore, unnecessary for the periphery of the state to offer such provision, as it is covered by external factions.

This is why it is generally true that the propagating factions external to the state—those developing in a postured manner with tangible input into the propagating system—will coincide with a decrepit state of the internal periphery. This also applies in the opposite case: if the internal periphery of the state provides the asset through severance and input into the central locale and its rumination, external factions will find themselves at odds regarding what development is necessary for input, since it is already being handled internally. In this sense, external factions will not be invested in the centric locale's article, because all systems are running smoothly. Whatever they might contribute is redundant, and they will value their own autonomy—operating independently of the entire system.

When external factions that depend on the political system's propagation express prominence or hostility toward the central political body, it is clear they are fulfilling needs to the internal system that are already addressed. Even though it should not be seen as hostility, but rather as prominence in providing assets to the central locale, hostility arises from the interpretation of that exposure.

Dynamics of Expansion and Global Engagement

This is where we enter into a more philosophical analysis. Expansion tends to extend further when the periphery of an internal faction does not provide a necessary asset to the central locale and its growth—thus signaling a call for justice to other entities, pushing such to its furthest reach until there is a response with the required provision.

In an ideal situation, the catalyst for expansion within central authority would only push the signal to the internal periphery of the state, as this is the closest and most logical source of the required provision. However, when the internal periphery cannot provide the necessary resources, the signal extends beyond the state, gradually pushing itself into the global sphere.

From a more practical standpoint, the structure of expansion itself does not change. Instead, external factions step in to provide the necessary provisions when the internal state fails to do so. When external factions intervene, they assume roles appointed by both the political body and the

The Structure of Consciousness

central authority, working toward the shared goal of ensuring expansion. In this context, the political body is tasked with disrupting the boundaries of the state, engaging in diplomacy with external factions to align them with the objective of facilitating growth.

It is almost as if the political body is hired to extend the state's boundaries, reaching to external factions, engaging in diplomacy, and initiating the expansion process. Once the internal factions assume responsibility for providing the needed provision, both the political body and the central authority will cease to request external assistance. However, external factions may still enter the process either by providing the missing provisions or contributing to the sequence in some way. Despite this, once the internal factions have taken responsibility, external factions will no longer be necessary, and each external faction will gain its autonomy— assuming the central authority and its structure are functioning effectively.

If we accept this proposition, where the structure remains unchanged, we must ask: what is the difference between a necessary provision granted to external factions and the meager effects of reflection upon their creation? We could argue that, without the call for action from central authority, central exposure itself holds no political significance for external factions. They would simply recognize the flow of events and continue maintaining their autonomy. They lose such, however, when the central authority begins issuing appointments external to the state. At that point, the once-autonomous political entities are pulled into the central process, responding to the *call to action*.

From this perspective, the signal itself does not change, but the reverberation within the signal alters the structure of external factions. Without the *call to action*, the signal can either be heard or ignored, depending on the choice of autonomous entities. Conversely, once the central authority issues a call, it becomes the most prominent signal, requiring a response. External factions must act accordingly.

As we know, hostility arises within external factions based on their interpretation of exposure and its *call to action*. Initially, they may interpret such as a loss of their autonomy, something most external political entities resist. This fear of losing autonomy fosters opposition. However, it is important to understand that central exposure is a natural reality. Autonomy does not stem from political devices alone, but from the fact that exposure is inherently structured. When that structure changes, the autonomy of external factions changes alongside it.

Additionally, external factions may interpret the *call to action* as an attempt to restructure their political organization. In the absence of a *call to action*, external political structures can construct themselves as they wish and remain bound by their traditional constitutions. However, when there is a *call to action*, exposure will affect the entire political structure, reconfiguring to align with the central locale, and thus be capable as an asset in providing consciousness sequence.

Conclusion: Constitutional Arbitriness and the Politics of Provision

If it remains in its traditional role, there is no semblance of a central locale, and thus no opportunity for individuals to engage in the development of consciousness that could eventually be reintegrated into the system. In this way, a full reconfiguration occurs—one that most autonomous political bodies neither support nor welcome, as it implies a reconstruction of their constitutions, almost as if those constitutions were arbitrary.

The truth is that all constitutions are, in essence, arbitrary; the purpose of a constitution is to protect exposure—and propagation, in turn, is only fair if it safeguards its central locales. This issue stems more from a misunderstanding of nature itself, and of the structural dynamics of political bodies, than from any practical dispute.

Political entities that do choose to respond to the *call for action*—to become facilitators of private consciousness development for reentry into the system—will ultimately find dissatisfaction if these provisions are sustained indefinitely. Once the internal periphery of the state reclaims this function, external states will lose access to the central authority and its process of propagation. At that point, they will be compelled to contribute significantly to ensure that the internal provisions are prioritized over anything that can be sourced externally.

PART V: CELEBRATION, TRAUMA, AND ENCAPSULATION

Celebration in Structuring Time and Memory

This categorization is not solely for the purpose of providing categories through which memories can interact with other memories; it serves a broader, more wholesome function. If its only purpose were to create distinctions, then any traumatic experience would serve the same role. Trauma would simply constitute a prior encapsulation, distinguishing post-trauma from pre-trauma, without offering relevance to the interactive experience itself.

Instead, trauma operates as a *shadow* space—an erratic zone of unconscious material, misdirection, and conformity—rather than a platform from which to engage in forward-looking thinking. Thus, we recognize two aspects of the interactive nature of celebration. First, it provides a distinct separation between two categories to enable dynamic exchange. As noted, any form of tragedy, disruption of consciousness, or conceptual burden can provide such nuance, shaping categorization.

Conversely, the second aspect cannot be related to trauma or general disruptions of consciousness, as this lack the intrinsic information required to shape the future or past. Trauma simply acts as a *shadow*, separating two distinct parts and creating a dynamic between categories. In contrast, the interactive experience of consciousness within celebration allows interaction itself to participate in a generality and wholeness that enables future dissemination from that bookmarked moment.

For example, a birthday separates and distinguishes years of life based on birth and individual growth. Yet it also provides an opportunity for a distinctive interactive experience that encapsulates consciousness at that instant. This encapsulation further offers material for future development. If categorization were purely about distinguishing time periods, it would lack interaction and become a chosen sentiment without existential significance.

Memory, Experience, and the Nature of Consciousness

When a birthday celebration becomes an interactive experience of consciousness, it acts as a capsule of selfhood that influences any forward-looking progress. This process allows previous experiences to be included and embedded in future ones. One might assume this is redundant—that if experiences were not separated and categorized, all previous information would naturally be included. However, the very act of separation creates a fissure, which necessitates an interactive encapsulation to carry information forward.

The nature of memory is such that, over time, if the psyche permits prolonged stretches of experience to remain unprocessed, the associated information gradually loses its vitality. As a result, one may fail to engage in forward-thinking and instead fade into the past, losing the ability to contribute evocatively to future-oriented thought. Categorization, when paired with interactive encapsulation, ensures that what might otherwise be forgotten becomes a generative force in future cognition.

An interactive experience requires defined parameters—a beginning and an end. When the beginning is undefined or the culmination lacks coherence, we are left with a "reality framework" instead of an interactive experience. The difference is that the former attempts to encapsulate the latter without the dynamic engagement necessary to sustain consciousness across time.

Dynamics and the Necessity of Temporal Distinctions in Consciousness

The reality framework is the orientation through which we perceive the world. If one were to celebrate unceasingly without distinct beginnings, endings, or periods of endurance, that framework would become their entire reality—offering no contrasting experience. The purpose of an interactive moment is its containment, allowing it to act as a counterpoint to general reality. A holiday provides structure to regular days just as the weekend balances the weekday. However, when a holiday extends beyond its intended timeframe, it loses its informative contrast and becomes the dominant reality. Even non-holiday moments may be perceived through the lens of that holiday framework.

A celebration that becomes too prolonged or malleable transforms into the prevailing reality. Those who then attempt to engage external to it begin interacting with the broader world as if it were an extension of that holiday framework. This shift is not merely about distinguishing between reality and interactive moments; it reflects a fundamental restructuring of the psyche. It is not just how much time is spent in each framework, but how the mind defines reality through those experiences.

The Psyche and Extended Interaction

The psyche does not automatically recognize an extended holiday as a reality framework unless it is approached as an interactive encapsulation that gradually expands until it reaches full consciousness. Consciousness evolves from cyclical interactive experiences that, over time, become accepted as the only reality. Once this shift occurs, and stipulating that it aligns with conscious parameters, the experience takes on a new character—not as something distinct from reality, but as the foundation for all other experiences.

One can, in theory, extend a holiday by treating it as a mirror interaction—an isolated experience, rather than an innovative reality. By keeping a contextual separation, one can continue engaging in the holiday essence while resisting the impulse to allow it to redefine their reality. Alternatively, one might engage with the holiday as a detached observer, experiencing it as a reactive encounter tied to a deeper source. However, this is difficult, as daily life creates structural links in the direction of consciousness that complicate such detachment.

To maintain this separation, one must convince the parameters of psyche that the experience is not reality but a constructed entity distinguished from it. This requires situating interactivity within an advanced form of reality that the psyche cannot manipulate. If the context extends into a reality already accepted by the psyche, it only reinforces and expands that framework. Just as building in a public domain shapes experience according to public norms, erection in a private domain creates a sheltered realm. How one positions interactivity determines its effect. The more public the inquiry, the more reality must be treated as its source material rather than an interactive platform.

The Limits of Simulation

The notion that all engagement with reality is merely a simulation—and that one can access a higher, more 'real' reality—is ultimately ineffective. The psyche recognizes reality as primary. Any prolonged, honest engagement with it reveals that such engagement must eventually transform one's understanding, making it unsustainable to continue viewing reality as merely simulated. Those who approach the 'central locale' (the primary space of consciousness) while treating it as a simulation can only do so temporarily. Sustained rumination and simulated interaction cannot coexist with genuine interactivity directed toward a higher realm.

This space—intended to inform a higher reality—cannot truly exist. It is not that there is nothing beyond the central locale, but rather that all things emanate from it. Anyone who engages deeply in its midst, whether from memory or in the case for which it is *centrally alive* will find themselves unable to interact with it in the same way again. Such individuals often move constantly, reconfiguring their perceptions to avoid vulnerability. In doing so, they avoid meeting reality as it is, and instead play psychological games to avoid fully confronting it.

If one insists on interacting with a reality to which they believe is structurally true, but does so through the lens of interactivity to proclaim a higher or better realm, they attach themselves to the more *shadow*y aspects of consciousness. They cannot ignore either the rumination or the reality of what it is. Rather than engaging with the vibrant aspects of experience, they interact with fragmented, vulnerable components—the periphery of consciousness.

Because the vulnerabilities of rumination reside in its *shadow*y elements, they can serve as a basis for interactivity—even if only from the periphery of consciousness. This form of interaction, however, is highly directive, fashioned entirely by the specific parameters of the *shadow* itself. It is not a personal engagement that emerges from a natural, open environment of interactivity—such as that found in the essence of celebration or holiday.

From an external vantage point, such engagement might appear interactive, but in truth, it is more akin to a championing of the psyche's vulnerabilities—as though these vulnerabilities were expressions of one's

Celebration in Structuring Time and Memory

personal, chosen interactivity. In reality, they represent the only available modes of engagement for personages who remain anchored in these *shadow*-laden locales. Their interaction is not born of personal preference or a deliberate move toward deeper reality, but from a condition in which no deeper reality exists for them.

They are exclusively embedded in the consciousness continuum, able to interact only with elements that have already lost substance within that cogitation. What results is not genuine interactivity but rather a recycling of the essence's exposed vulnerabilities. In effect, they become part of the *shadow* itself—a participant in the *shadow* of consciousness propagation. This occurs without any true interactivity or active participation in the exposure itself, at least not in a way that aligns with their full intellectual or experiential capacity outside of such advocacy.

Categorization and Encapsulation in Celebrations and Trauma

Through the interactive experience of celebration—such as a birthday—one creates an interaction that brings nuance to the coming year. This ensures the previous year continues implicitly. Without celebration, and without the fissures of consciousness that create categorization, the past loses vitality. As time, place, and memory stretch, they become skeletal, diminishing the substance of experience.

Categorization, by creating distinct phases, enables interactive experiences that encapsulate the past within a specific time and space, imprinting it upon the psyche. This process allows information to be disseminated in real-time. This is analogous to having a child: the experience creates a clear "before" and "after" due to the depth of exposure it introduces. The interactive experience of early parenthood allows engagement with one's prior self from a new, grounded place. More broadly, children always represent the previous stage of a parent's life up to the point of their arrival. Because this transition is deeply interactive, it enriches the past rather than permitting it fade into obscurity.

The Makeup of Celebrations and Trauma

A celebration consists of two essential elements: (1) the categorical partialization of what came before and what comes after, and (2) the interactive experience that encapsulates the consciousness of the prior category. When one of these is missing, the event assumes a different character.

Trauma, for instance, consists mainly of categorization, with some degree of encapsulation—but of a fragmented, rather than inclusive, nature. This imbalance makes trauma difficult to process. It cannot function as a cohesive encapsulation like celebration, yet it remains vital for continuity of selfhood.

The challenge of trauma is to manage such without fully engaging or entirely dismissing of it. Both extremes are detrimental to psyche coherence: full engagement validates such as an encapsulation, while dismissal erases part of one's history. Trauma requisites to be acknowledged without being allowed to dominate. In contrast, celebrations aim to encapsulate experience into a meaningful whole. Trauma isolates an extreme point along the continuum of experience.

Intimacy and Ritual

Another case where only one element is present is in non-ritualized intimacy. In such instances, there is encapsulation of a specific moment, but no categorization to place it within a broader continuum. As a result, this intimacy becomes fragmented, contributing to personal growth in an erratic method. Without a categorical framework, it cannot be part of a structured progression. It remains an inconsistent interactive arrangement where experiences are encapsulated without continuity.

Ritualized intimacy, such as anniversaries, includes both categorization and encapsulation when properly structured. This ensures continuity and reinforces the relationship through defined parameters. Without both elements, intimacy remains sporadic rather than contributing to a sustained developmental arc.

The Convergence of Consciousness and the Holiday Experience

Once these two elements—categorization and encapsulation—are established, we can see their foundational role in celebrations and holidays. Categorization is most commonly associated with time, as it effectively separates conscious experiences without redundancy. The division of time into years, rather than months, weeks, or days, allows for a distinct separation of conscious phases. Seasons also serve as natural categorizations, occurring four times a year in a consistent cycle that prevents redundancy. For this reason, most celebrations or holidays are tied to the calendar or seasonal cycles.

Another form of categorization is the personalization of consciousness. Regardless of the occasion, it is marked by the year or season, allowing it to interact dynamically with the present era. Some categorizations are not meant to be repeated but rather serve to separate major life stages. These often include a significant event—such as a change in location, a transformative experience, or another restructuring—that naturally creates a separation. In these cases, encapsulation is required to allow the new period to interact implicitly with what preceded it. This is achieved through a highly interactive experience that embeds the transition into the psyche.

Conversely, experiences that involve encapsulation without categorization—such as spontaneous intimacy or telling but unstructured experiences—require categorization to achieve continuity. Marriage serves as the pivotal juncture, a change of residence, career, or other restructure that will have the effect of categorization. In these cases, what is required is not categorization, for that appears naturally, but encapsulation, so that the period can interact once the differentiation takes effect, through the means of a highly interactive moment that is usually the cause for embeddedness of the psyche.

The opposite is true too, in which there may be an experience of intimacy or other form in which there is an encapsulation, which thus requires categorization to provide the full effect of that interaction. Thus, we find that marriage serves to categorize amorousness and its interactive aspects, meaning that everything preceding marriage does not belong to the same category and must instead rely on the interactive encapsulation of the romance that marriage defines. This does not disallow further interactive encapsulations; though, they too must be categorized if they are going to take the effect of continuity.

The Risk of Mischaracterization in Celebration

A celebration can lose its encapsulating function and instead become a characterization, failing to provide an interactive connection to the prior state. This shift can occur if an individual experiences a negative impact or traumatic event during the celebration. Because they are open to the interactive experience at that moment, the experience may deviate from encapsulation and instead *contrast* with the intended meaning.

We would always find sympathy with the individual that is enduring certain implicit celebratory events or holidays, continuing as an alternative of the encapsulation and interactive experience that exposes them to the negative side and the trauma of its elements. Had they not attended to the parameters necessary for animating a celebratory exposure, they would have remained susceptible to falling into its *contrast* rather than achieving its encapsulation. For to truly encapsulate something, one must allow themselves full availability and exposure to all its elements. It follows, then, that such openness renders one perceptively available to any formalization of reality—including a descent into that very reality.

Encapsulation and Traumatic Exposure

Traumatic exposure occurs when one has already been presented for a particular interaction or experience, only for it to deviate from its expected course. Without the attempted availability of celebratory notions to encapsulate elements, traumatic exposure lacks credibility as a defining event. One often expects a certain level of trauma and positions themselves advantageously to surpass that threshold—only to fail.

This is evident, for example, in warfare. When trauma arrives without one's prior awareness of the exposure, they are placed at the horizon of encapsulating a momentary state before the ordeal itself. We often fail to recognize that every traumatic instance has a preceding state in which one attempts encapsulation, only to fail as the trauma unfolds. Whether the trauma is anticipated for seconds or moments, individuals expose themselves to reality with the hope of a celebratory experience or interactive exposure. However, instead of achieving this, they decline into negativity—a *contrast* to their intended exposure.

The Nature of Encapsulation

The central argument is that when one seeks to encapsulate the full experience of consciousness—whether in a holiday or celebratory event or in its antithesis of trauma— they initially attempt to embrace the full encapsulation of experience. However, this effort can lead to deviation, where instead of being exposed to individuality contained by nature, one loses such altogether. The *contrast* of experience is not merely a formalization of negativity but an encapsulation of reality devoid of its parameters, absorbing the dimmer aspects of existence.

Reality can be perceived from two perspectives: [1] as a structured platform. [2] As a state of nothingness, emptiness, and vanity.

For instance, if someone feels responsible for another but fails, they may encapsulate that inability in providing. Reality remains as it is, but they internalize such as confirmation of failure. Similarly, with survivor's guilt, one encapsulates the renunciation inherent in the fact that some survive while others do not, internalizing a reality defined by *contrast* rather than continuity.

Categorization and the Loss of Encapsulation

If one were to compile a list of the natural limitations and problems of reality, it would reveal that those who encapsulate experience through *contrast* follow a structured order, deprived of true nuance or deviation. This demonstrates that an encapsulation is not merely an individual experience but a philosophical perspective upon reality, made possible by its limitations.

However, the encapsulation of a composite experience of consciousness always varies and is nuanced, because it is willing to expose oneself to all its elements, not merely by *contrast*s. This philosophical inquiry into the limitations of nature will lead to a few key problems: exposure to reality through encapsulation will reveal a very individual process toward consciousness, which is not universally clear. Just as consciousness evolves over time, becoming more complex and nuanced, so too does the interactive exposure through encapsulation. While there may be general themes, they will not be universal in nature. Instead, we find great interest in the diverse stories that encapsulation reveals.

As noted, encapsulation can occur without categorization, which provides only meager provision for forward-looking sentiment because it does not distinguish two parts of a whole. Traumatic instances will naturally generate a categorization by disrupting a conscious flow for an extended period, marking a dramatic event that is "bookmarked" in time.

A celebratory occasion, however, might not descend into the same categorization if one were not to distinguish it as a medium of satisfaction, separate from the reality beyond it. This is especially true if the celebration is prolonged over a day, week, or even month, as it becomes impossible to categorize due to over-stimulation. The effect of losing categorization is that, if a moment is not appreciated and distinguished for itself, it loses both categorization and encapsulation.

How could one be exposed to a stream of reality for an entire month? More importantly, how could one distinguish that month from the rest of the year? Something that could have a dynamic impact must be momentary, encapsulated in a way that gives it distinct character, as though we understand its personality. (Although horoscopes give such detail, it is already otherworldly in being too general of a category, with a lack of

The Convergence of Consciousness and the Holiday Experience

empirical data[8]) We cannot know the personality of a month or the character of its composition but rather we could distinguish moments as such and therefore cataloguing a moment is treated as a standalone experience that is meant to expire and does not begin until it pronounces itself. A key principle of encapsulation is that a moment must be momentary. It must be distinct, defined, and finite. We cannot attribute personality or character to an entire month; nevertheless we can understand individual moments with clear identities. Proper categorization allows encapsulation to function effectively. If an experience is overextended, it loses both categorization and encapsulation.

The Vulnerabilities of Continuous Encapsulation

Another vulnerability of a lack of categorization is the inability to encapsulate properly. Relying on a continuum of consciousness weakens the encapsulation process, making it futile or insufficient. One only gains entrance into an interactive platform when they are absent from it; if it is constantly sought, it will provide only liminal encapsulations of satisfaction.

The reason for this is that one essentials a strong reality framework to gain the insight necessary for encapsulating a momentary experience. Each attempt at encapsulating will outdo the prior one, as it disperses its information. This leads to the false assumption that the encapsulation itself is reality, rather than an informant of reality. The present attempt at encapsulation will always undermine the prior one, leaving the previous encapsulation as immaterial. This is how extended intimacy leads to a deterioration of intimacy—each successive moment of encapsulation competes with the previous, and eventually, the entire process of encapsulation seems insufficient so that the impression becomes one where both reality and its encapsulation are seen as insufficient markers of evocative attention. In some sense this is why overextended intimacy results in a nihilistic undertone: extended intimacy denies the reality that

---

[8] Shawn Carlson's 1985 Nature study subjected 28 professional astrologers to blind chart-matching trials: none could match birth-chart profiles to psychological inventories better than chance (Carlson 1985) The protocol—vetted in advance by both physicists and astrologers—eliminated selection and confirmation bias, yet the results "clearly refute the astrological hypothesis", Carlson, Shawn, *A Double-Blind Test of Astrology*. Nature.

The Structure of Consciousness

has been gained, and its continual extension argues against the psyche, suggesting that reality is never sufficient.

Returning to the subject at hand, a celebratory moment can deviate in the direction of being a *contrast* to reality instead of an engagement to encapsulate reality. A negative inference is not necessarily the exchange of *contrast*, and therefore, should not be considered virginally celebratory. It is the perception of that *contrast* in which one attempts to encapsulate, despite its loss. This is the difference between the sacrificial element that culminates to be a complete renunciation instead of it being a mere *contrast* to a reality engagement that is wholesome and encapsulating.

The key difference of being an encapsulation as opposed to a *contrast* is based on the inclusion of the whole picture despite the prevalent *contrast*. Usually, in cases where a celebratory moment does not contain a significant degree of *contrast*, the attainment of encapsulation becomes more prevalent. However, the nature of individuals is such that once they are exposed to an interactive platform—through the encapsulation of all of reality—a natural manifestation of psychological resistance, often represented by *contrast*, will emerge. As a result, encapsulation is still required despite this resistance. This is only in the case in which one seeks that celebratory experience so that if it is ignored or not relegated to such an interactive platform, then it would have the *contrast* make out itself.

For example, in a wedding, although the general notion is celebratory, we often observe a manifestation of *contrast*—one's perceptual reality questions the nature of the event, especially in those who seek the celebratory experience. It is not that they are unappreciative or doubtful, but that, through their exposure, they notice the *shadow* in the backdrop of reality, which has the potential to manifest. Even so, the quest for and encapsulation of both the experience and the endeavor will outweigh the *contrast*.

In traumatic instances, the *contrast* makes itself known to such an extent that encapsulating beyond it becomes less prevalent. The individual may descent into encapsulating the *contrast* itself, instead of seeing beyond it. There is a momentary glance when one engages with the *contrast* through a traumatic instance, in which they notice the full scope of reality and the potential for encapsulation. However, this is ignored in favor of the event's *contrast*.

When categorization is weak, encapsulation becomes unstable. Consciousness relies on a structured framework to maintain meaningful interactive experiences. Overextending encapsulation results in diminishing returns, as each attempt to encapsulate a moment surpasses the previous one, rendering it insufficient.

Each successive moment of encapsulation competes with the last; leading to the perception that reality itself is inadequate. This is why overextended intimacy results in its own decline—continuous encapsulation fosters the belief that reality is never sufficient. The repeated attempt to encapsulate reality eventually leads to a nihilistic undertone, as reality and its encapsulation are seen as inadequate markers of meaningful attention.

Encapsulation and Contrast

Returning to our primary argument: a celebratory moment can either engage reality or become its *contrast*. A negative inference does not inherently *contrast* with reality but instead represents an attempt to encapsulate, despite loss. This distinction separates a mere renunciation from an active engagement with reality.

Encapsulation involves incorporating the entire picture, even if *contrast*s are present. In celebratory moments, the majority of the experience is not *contrast*-based, allowing for successful encapsulation. However, individuals who actively engage in a full spectrum of reality often encounter *contrast*s naturally. This phenomenon is particularly noticeable during weddings, where the overarching mood is celebratory, yet individualistic experiences may surface underlying *contrast*s. Those seeking to fully obtain the celebratory experience may simultaneously recognize the "*shadow*" of reality in the background.

It is not that they doubt or dismiss the occasion, but through deep exposure, they become aware of its *contrast*. However, because the act of encapsulating both the event and experience outweighs the *contrast*, the moment remains celebratory. In traumatic instances, the *contrast* dominates, making it difficult to see beyond it. Even though there is a brief moment in which one sees the entire scope of reality and the possibility of encapsulation, often this is overlooked in favor of fixating on the *contrast* itself.

PART VI: INTEGRATION, COLLAPSE, AND THE EDGE OF CONSCIOUS SYSTEMS

The Interaction between Structure and Streamline Consciousness

The convergence of consciousness involves the interplay between two simultaneous processes, each defined either by differentiation or by convergence. The first process is the *streamline consciousness*, which is not necessarily actualized but represents an amendment to personhood. The second is the *structured state*, which refers to the baseline individual and their rudimentary condition. These two realms—the structured individual and the streamline consciousness—do not always converge; the baseline state remains a premise, while streamline consciousness serves as an ideal that may not always integrate with the system.

It is possible that the structured system is unavailable during the exploration of consciousness, as the latter operates in the realm of material and does not seek to actualize a form that suffices for the individual. In this scenario, the two realms may intertwine, with one aspect of consciousness explored at the expense of its actualization, while the structured realm is activated in contradiction of the idea of higher development.

When engaging in platforming or in an interactive state, what is actually happening is a merging of the structured realm with a form of consciousness. This process of *mending* is a convergence of two distinct realms at odds with each other. Thus, there must be a leap from the structured, interactive realm to streamline consciousness, since the structured realm cannot comprehend anything beyond its substance or orientation. The ability for this convergence is through a vulnerability in which the entire structured system becomes open and available to its fundamental state in question, so that it can interact with the streamline of consciousness.

Because of this, for a momentary state, there is to be considered a zero-realm interaction because the structure is lost to availability, and the streamline consciousness has not yet been integrated. In this exposed state, it is fairly possible that instead of one reaching beyond the structured realm, one falls into existential vulnerability thereby denouncing the entire process.

This leap can only occur through vulnerability, where the entire structured system becomes open to its fundamental state, allowing it to interact with streamline consciousness. In this exposed state, it is possible that instead of moving beyond the structured realm, one may fall into existential vulnerability and abandon the process altogether.

The experience of merging consciousness with the structured realm is disingenuous, because the structured realm cannot extend beyond its parameters. The only form of expansion it can achieve is through personality differentiation, where one dissociates from the structure's demands to seek something beyond it. In this case, the structured realm loses its attachment, and consciousness becomes devoid of real actualization. Instead, actualization occurs through inference, where the structured realm continues trying to engage even as it is diminished from purview, and at some point, a meaningful engagement between consciousness and the structured realm happens.

The only reason there is structured engagement with streamline consciousness is that a certain platform of individuality is required to endure the interaction. Initially, engagement is not achieved through these methods, but rather through a leap from the structured realm into streamline consciousness, using the structured realm merely as an orienting backdrop. It is as though one betrays a friend, yet still brings them into a new social

The Interaction between Structure and Streamline Consciousness

context, as the sympathetic familiarity manifests, despite the betrayal. Without the betrayal of the structured realm, the ability to access streamline consciousness would not exist.

Once engagement with streamline consciousness begins, the structured realm that arrives is not of the same orientation as the genuine structured realm. Instead, one recreates the structured realm in their imagination—similar to the friendship that one brings along into a new social sphere, which is not the true nature of friendship but only what is understood and reimagined for forward purpose. If we are to follow the true nature of this process, the new sphere of sociality influences the entire orientation of one's perception of their prior friendship. This is also the case with the connection to streamline consciousness: even as one presumes to bring along the structured realm and its interactive baseline, it is only an imagination of that factual nature. If we study the two realms—the one brought into consciousness and the one relegated in real-time—they are wholly different, substantiated, and very distinct forms.

The reason we cannot include the material structured reality is because, once there is engagement with the streamline consciousness, we no longer have stabilization and access to structured reality. An attempt to bridge genuine structured reality with streamline consciousness will only create dissent toward consciousness, since the structured reality will perceive the idolization of streamline consciousness as a disingenuous formation, not rooted in anything material. Every attempt at convergence will send the conscious substance to its corner to reveal that it is a matter of imitation rather than a form to be reckoned with.

Therefore, we must detach from structured reality before any engagement with the consciousness realm. Once the engagement commences, there is a recreation of the structured realm to assist with individuality and perspective. This recreated realm, being composed of consciousness, is more directly connected to it than to structured reality. It only has the presence of alignment per structured reality since that is the direction of the individual, but the details and parameters are configured for consciousness association.

At this point, there is a possibility of convergence between the recreated structured realm and the newfound consciousness, as they are of the same source, with only the imagination of the individual as their separator. The converged material can then be placed upon the psyche for further interaction once one departs from the consciousness realm and enters genuine structured reality. At that point, one will engage at the baseline level, only to become aware of this other realm that is similar but deviates at certain intervals.

The Slow Infusion: How Consciousness Becomes Structured Reality

With the plot set in motion, over time the discrepancy may not be noticed outright. Instead, assumptions will lead to genuine convergence based on similarity and parallels. It is at this point that structured reality gains true convergence, which can be considered an indirect input from streamlined consciousness. This is the manner in which structured reality becomes consciously infused—so that through a sleight of hand, it advances and progresses. Once there is integration, these consciousness notions are considered structured reality and become part of the baseline of the individual. Because the baseline is bound to the parameters of the biological system, anything entered, which is adversarial to biological inference, will eventually fade out.

For example, general hygiene that has advanced in the contemporary era and restroom procedure and ritual has become structured reality in a short time. This is because the inputted material of structured reality did not meet opposition, as the biological realm decided with those suppositions. Unless one is threatened with insanity, they will not diverge from this hygienic progress in structured reality, even though its development originated as an external consciousness parameter. There is little to teach or learn to follow the hygienic process because it has been so successful, recording as natural as the very air we breathe. We owe the process to a lack of adversarial notions after the input, almost as if the biological system has noted, "What took you so long"—since it meets all the parameters of its system. However, it was not the system that arrived at these conclusions but rather a conscious inquiry that followed the process we mentioned. Only that the biological system agrees wholeheartedly to the change, even though it did not participate in the development.

This is why, despite all the enjoyment of this process, if elements are received that prove adversarial to the biological system, they will be thwarted over time. It is these elements that require continuous reengagement because they fade with time and biological resistance. For example, holiday rituals are to be considered a necessary re-implementation because they are not aligned with the biological system. The holiday ritual

The Interaction between Structure and Streamline Consciousness

is a composition of conscious substance that is permeating from streamlined consciousness.

The ritual aspect is only to engineer the recreation of the structured reality in a new form for conscious convergence. After the fact, when we gain a convergence between the ritualized reality and consciousness, the reception of structured reality will be convinced of their similarities and begin the genuine convergence. However, because conscious substance was based on a contextual overlay that does not perfectly align with biological parameters, the convergence will find itself halted in structured reality. This is why a developed holiday must reach into a streamline of consciousness that is aligned with universality and more so with biological parameters.

For illustration, holidays that are centered on the winter season must be continually reintegrated because the convergence with biological parameters is not forthcoming. While it may be a notion to embrace the winter season, the biological perception of winter and its cold is a limitation upon the system rather than a necessity. One can survive and progress without winter—it is an impediment upon the individual when it occurs. One can embrace biological impediments, but they will never be considered structured reality. Therefore, the implementation of holidays related to the winter season will requisite to be reintegrated regularly, because the convergence will eventually fade. We notice that there was a history of holidays that, through succession and convergence without biological adversarial notions, have become ingrained into structured reality, to the point that there is no longer a need for the holiday. For specimen, the seasons of spring, summer, and autumn have already been imprinted into structured reality, and any semblance of a need for a holiday in those markers is due to a need for categorization, not convergence.

Any civilized individual intuitively is made aware of a consciousness for spring, summer, and autumn, and it is such because of the work that has been done in history. We assume that the reason we are aware of this consciousness—the flower blossom of spring, the sociality of summer, and the dwindling of autumn—is because these are social events. Rather, the reason is that the social realm understands these elements, and as we watch, we notice a very strict regimen of interaction in accordance with those understandings.

We will find scarcely individuals who arrive at the seashore during early spring or autumn, even as the weather is not necessarily of different proportions, and this is not done by any law or even social cue. This is based on an understanding of these elements, so that each aspect will participate according to its consciousness level. More so than a ritual, it is embedded into structural reality. The only requirement of these seasons is the categorization, which is made possible by holidays that do not substantiate consciousness attachment and instead serve as bookmarks. When we notice the prevalence of a holiday, we can either determine that the consciousness is not universal, is in the process of being implemented, or there are biological constraints.

For example, *New Years* is a holiday that is in the process of being implemented at full scale without a biological impediment. The biological system agrees with the premise of configuring a major categorization between aspects of its prior state, so that any holiday which premises categorization will retain a certain relevance despite its other attachments. The transitory prominence for the biological system is one that is fairly significant and will be individuated.

We can assume that eventually the notion of a need for holidays related to categorization will no longer be necessary, as that will be part of structured reality—so much so that it would be as simple as waking in the morning, to create and formulate categorizations according to the personal regulation of their development. If we are to analyze, most of holiday relevance in the contemporary era is based on categorization, presently to be a public exemplification, but at a later date to become a personal premise based on the constitutions of individuals.

Thus, one would have their personal "New Year" based on their development, and the very notion of sociality being different is of no consequence because it is intuitively grounded. As of yet, this is not the case, so that it requires a public proclamation for such to take effect.

The next evolution of holidays will be afforded either to the reimplementation of non-biologically-agreeing aspects or new consciousness aspects that could be implemented into the structure of reality. We could question the first premise—if it is not biologically confounded, then why promote its prevalence, being that it goes against the very notion of structured reality?

This is because there will always be elements important for consciousness—for the very maintenance of consciousness—which are not meant for convergence but exist solely to give vitality to the consciousness process itself. For these, the continued holiday tradition that ensures such benefits will be enabled, even as the promise of convergence is not there.

The Interaction between Structure and Streamline Consciousness

Although these are not the fundamental holidays for the objective of development, they are to ensure that development can occur in the future.

Therefore, the experience of convergence is to be considered at two distinct points. The first is the recreated reality for the objective of streamlining consciousness, and the second is the regularity of structural reality to which converged consciousness sentiment becomes regulated by that system.

Activation vs. Convergence: When Reality Misses Itself

The second point is not a convergence, as two linear lines might meet, but more like two parallel lines that are compelled to borrow from each other for their similarities. We will term the first point as *convergence* and the second as the *activation*.

The activation is a circumstance that is not simulated, for structural reality continues as it would, with only the effect of its forced deviation with the second parallel line. It is more considered a mistake of circumstance, to which entrapment has structural reality unable to discern itself and thus become more than itself.

This is why a very firm adherence to structural reality will make activation impossible, as one will notice any dissimilar attributes, including that second parallel line. Therefore, part of activation is a sort of detachment or disability with the entire structural experience, so that in the lapses, it can activate the similar linear lines.

We will notice those who perform the lapse in perfect time, and because of this, it would not be a structural activation but rather a conscious effort at convergence. Instead, the dis-adherence to structural reality stems from the consideration of different experiences that are not set in stone like that of structural reality. As well, the presumed structural reality can be differentiated from true nature, so that one who adheres too thoroughly has less of a hold on its premise, for the reason that they are not available for their personal discrepancies.

The point of the matter is that the activation of two parallel lines is not a simulated effect but a change of structure through similarities. The simulation is only in effect when one engages with consciousness so that the recreation of structural reality for its premise is completely simulated and does not disclose a real semblance of genuine reality—only enough to convince the psyche and sociality of its surface appearance, while the rest of its construction is merely a repositioning of consciousness material into that mold.

This is why we cannot endure a holiday or celebration as structural reality—because it is a consciousness effort—and the structural reality that does seem to fit is but a recreation.

The perfect form of a holiday or celebration is when the consciousness material is universal, the recreation of structural reality is genuine to reality, and the convergence includes biological parameters. First off, the lists of acceptable holidays or celebrations are those that engage with specific contexts instead of a universal engagement of themes and natural social development.

If it has to maintain a distinct sociality or does not clearly follow universal themes, then it provides a consciousness that is not aligned with systemic consciousness and thus only distances from a lasting convergence, causing misalignment between universality and social universality.

The second cause of imperfect convergence is the recreation of structural reality. When this is done in a way that preserves the consciousness sentiment in contradiction of the task of recreating reality, then—even with convergence—it will not parallel an activation, since the genuine structural reality does not find it to be similar. This can occur from a focus on consciousness instead of a two-party convergence, where structural reality is not given autonomy in its creation. This happens when one does not understand genuine structural reality, so that a recreation only causes it to drift further from the genuine premise.

Consciousness in Retreat and Social Disintegration

With some ironic realization, it can be said that the conscious system embraces a form that goes contrary to its suppositions. The holiday is the activation of a domesticated process, so that during this interval, consciousness is not streamlined. Internal to that very conscious system, it disrupts itself to go contrary to its structure, so that there is attenuation to that interactivity which makes for a better form for later consciousness endeavors.

We can consider it to be a complete renunciation of the entire system, so that it performs the very disintegration that would even disallow the activation of the supposition towards the holiday; almost like a fading interaction. By the time the holiday is through and consciousness is lost,

The Interaction between Structure and Streamline Consciousness

interactivity is at its highest, so that there is a hopeful mending process that would allow reintegration and reformation of consciousness.

The ability to perform such a feat requires a contextual overlay. Without it, it would not be able to be a social agreement, since there is nothing of the system to dispel it. There is no internal mechanism for such an activation and it requisites an uncommon contextual overlay which directs the entire system. Since the system espouses universality, which would be lost had it ever entered into a contextual agreement; the system relies on something universal for its contextual output. That is the season, for which the very engagement of disengagement that arrives with *winter* disrupts a sequential pattern between sociality and makes for an individual to enter into themselves. That very season is used as a contextual footprint for this endeavor.

Despite contrary suppositions, the winter season does not require to disintegrate a consciousness system, although it is far more difficult to maintain. So instead of driving the maintenance of the consciousness system throughout, there is a contextual usage of that very habitat which causes the utilization of the consciousness system to dispel itself. "When maintenance is scarce, and the holiday 'spirit' is lacking, there is an attempt to sustain the consciousness continuum throughout the season. However, since the contextual output is agreed upon by most of sociality, general consciousness is to dispel itself and downgrade to an interactive embodiment, much like their subsidiaries.

Differing from the subsidiaries, which correct an earlier notion, it does not downgrade in a genuine format but only utilizes the system itself to downgrade, although remaining as it were the entire time. At the height of the holiday, consciousness remains but is most potent to dispel itself into interactivity instead of its true nature. One can attend to the consciousness system as a regularity but will find that the contextual output engineered into each attempt is met with a loss of individuality, since that very system espouses to downgrade, including anyone who attempts normal interaction. Rather, the only method of proper interaction is to engage with that locale as interactive embodiment, as discussed in other works.[9]

One of the major elements of a consciousness system is the social agreement, and when a majority, especially the most important constituents, become participants in this social agreement, it becomes impossible to gain

---

[9] *Philosophy of the Center of Civilization*, Baruch Menache, (2024).

The Structure of Consciousness

entry into the system through normal affairs and only in its interactive embodiment element.

At most, there is going to be a representation of domestication, as a mechanism to assist in the experience of interactivity, and this may be the only permeation of consciousness during the holiday interval. This representation is given credence to follow against the normal parameters of the interactive embodiment because it becomes the portal between the interactive system and consciousness itself. Similarly, an embodied interactive system has a portal through which it receives and disseminates consciousness, even though it has strict parameters to keep it separate from consciousness. The consciousness system cannot simply downgrade to *interactive* without offering a consciousness portal between itself and the downgraded system.

If we examine this further, we find that the conscious system does not truly disappear but instead retreats into individuality, protected by a social agreement that keeps it hidden within interactivity. If consciousness were to dissipate entirely, reintegration would be impossible, as it would be genuinely lost. Instead, consciousness exists in reserve between individuals, continuously re-approaching its expression without full exposure. This process hinges on context. As long as individuals retain context—especially within their personal consciousness—they are neither fully redirected by interactivity nor excessively exposed in ways that disrupt the social flow. Thus, consciousness remains available even when the social agreement dictates otherwise.

The latter problem of reception might be a greater deficiency, for then we are enabling a decorum of consciousness to permeate individuals, allowing them to reach a state of actualization. The problem with individual actualization that lacks the support of society or the structural system is that one becomes trapped within the encapsulation of that experience. By exposing consciousness, individuals end up creating bubbles that will be used incorrectly. This is the ostensible lonesome experience for individuals who participate in a conscious system when it is demanding disintegration, so they are left unfounded as a sole individual on an island and in a representational format. This is the most truly lonesome state, for genuine loneliness without representational agreement is only experienced in so much as one represents themselves. But if one is participating in a habitat that represents its disintegration all while attempting to go against that will, they will experience a true state of loneliness.

The question that arises, then, is whether a conscious realm can retain its status despite its temporary disintegration. If there is a social agreement toward this downgraded process, is it solely the responsibility of individuals to reintegrate consciousness?

Celebration and the Conscious System

In some sense, celebration is contrary to the entire conscious system because one can only reflect or to detach from it. Only then does the system itself become a declaration: celebrating itself despite its intrinsic nature as a sequence of consciousness. Individuals, too, may celebrate by stepping away from conscious discrimination, entering a kind of downgrade that manifests as an interactive structure. This is distinct from participation in a corporeal structure and stands apart from the overwhelming experience of consciousness. It is not inherently a demotion, but rather a participation in an inversely oriented structure.

Proper celebration is the continued participation in a conscious endeavor, but only by choice—whether that of the individual or society. The structure of this choice reflects an adversarial nature: for society, it is the choice to de-participate from participation; for the individual, it is the choice to emphasize the interactive experience over the conscious sequence. Since individuals rely upon society for the procedural conditions of participation, they are bound by locational circumstances. If one resides within a realm of consciousness that does not seek to disseminate or de-participate, they will not have the ability to participate interactively, and thus cannot create an interactive environment—because that is not the true nature of the surrounding environment.

For instance, during seasonal proceedings where consciousness does not choose to downgrade itself, an individual cannot participate interactively as if the environment were in fact interactive—because that is not the true nature of that political realm. If one attempt anyhow, they enter into an actualization of themselves as a *shadow* of that environment. The individual becomes an emphasis of interactivity whereas the environment does not seek such, thus demonstrating vulnerability instead of regulation. The same can be said for an environment that chooses to downgrade: if an individual continues to participate as if it were a conscious sequence, they

The Structure of Consciousness

merely actualize the interactive embodiment, which is fundamentally experienced as though it were a consciousness sequence. (e.g., loneliness)

As emphasized elsewhere, an individual who wishes their participation must adapt to the environment that aligns with that circumstance. Therefore, if one is participating in a conscious expanse which seeks to engage in a corporeal experience alongside supplementary interactivity, they must materially depart from that environment, entering into a corporeal atmosphere. However, because of this choice, the corporeal environment is habitually not interactive, but instead with slight monumentality. If one wants to participate in a proper interactive environment, the only path of entry is to materially attach to a conscious sequence which selects to downgrade itself. No other realm would offer such an atmosphere, because any corporeal system or interactive structure will lose itself as a permeation of direct consciousness, becoming instead, a regular interactive structure.

If the corporeal system wishes to participate through embodiment, it must answer to the relevance of the surrounding environment. If the environment is propagating as a conscious sequence, it only participates as a domain for that; and if it chooses to participate as an interactive system, it does so as the *shadow* of that environment. To be an interactive system which does not acknowledge the *shadow* of that environment, it must separate itself from that expansion and remain concealed; but still would be an ascendancy of that environment.

As noted elsewhere, an attempted interactive system contained by the expansion of a conscious sequence will automatically participate in that sequence, whether for stout interactivity or consciousness, which can either be the *shadow* or a host that interacts with that system. This is why the secretive domain within a consciousness expansion will always be a *shadow* and never perform as an interactive experience.

Unless the physical domain actively chooses to be interactive, it cannot serve as an interactive environment. According to our analysis, when the conscious sequence refuses to demote to an interactive form, no domain can perform as one. Any domain attempting to be interactive under such conditions will become either a host or a *shadow*. Those outside the first-tier boundaries of participation will experience interactivity without embodiment. The only true interactive embodiment is available when the environment itself has chosen to become interactive. That is why the

The Interaction between Structure and Streamline Consciousness

interactive environment is of critical importance to the conscious system, it alone holds no affiliation to anything but itself.

The primary benefit of an interactive environment is the conscious experience of elementary levels of one's development. An interactive system that is not embodied cannot be fully experienced through embodiment and therefore is not consciously connected. Only in the interactive environment is one able to participate in the rudimentary stage of their conscious development without demoting that development in the future. Obviously, we require a contextual bridge to avoid arriving to that interactive environment as an actualization, but only as a context from the conscious helm to that embodiment; so it doesn't lose itself but also gains the prerogative of conscious leadership of the elementary levels of development.

I cannot emphasize enough the importance of interactive embodiment. Without it—prolonged for an extended period—one would either lose attachment to their developmental stage of consciousness or actualize its realm at the expense of later developments. Even as losing attachment to earlier frameworks of consciousness echoes as unassuming, it is not. Without attachment to one's conscious development as a sequence, they will begin to perform according to the necessities of earlier consciousness levels. There is a need for the fulfillment of consciousness at these reduced modality levels. In the direction of one's consciousness leadership, will inevitably have one participate in these uncomplicated levels as a subconscious layer, redirecting themselves to those earlier stages. The social ramifications are complex, and if a society performs such for a long interval, it will degrade itself to a fundamental state.

To return to the topic at hand: the importance of celebration is paramount for this union. Either the individual enters interactivity—or, preferably, embodied interactivity—or society seeks to disseminate its conscious sentiment to function as an interactive structure. It is almost as though the consciousness sequence seeks to domesticate itself, just as individuals seek to domesticate themselves. However, not all domestications are the same. Most result in erratic interactivity that does not link directly to consciousness, and thus cannot perform as a conscious experience.

This is not to say that any domestication lacking embodiment lacks formal purpose for the conscious system. Rather, domestication without embodiment serves only as a prerequisite to a textual overlay—performed once attaching to a conscious system for embodiment. This is why familial domestication is never enough of a domain of domestication: it must either be directly linked to consciousness (if the domain is settled and conscious), or an interactive experience without such a link. This does not negate the value of non-embodied domestication, but rather shows that it is within this realm that one gains access to the elementary tiers of domestication, which can evolve into a more advanced theory of embodied domestication.

There is a type of domestication required of all individuals: first, to partake effectively in an interactive environment; and second, to domesticate their private undertakings in order to join in at higher levels. Not everything in the psyche requires a consciousness sequence—only the formulated elements that have already been personally engaged and now demand a degree of embodiment. For example, one must interactively appropriate childhood states, even while existing in adult form. They might gain embodiment for participation in an *interactive embodied environment* through a contextual bridge from their conscious leadership to that realm. However, there is also a need to domesticate childhood permeations that do not require embodiment, but rather domesticity of their inner affairs.

This is done by allowing interactivity to sequence itself external to the consciousness sequence—allowing those experiences to be formulated from childhood sentiments. When the time for embodiment arrives, they can be performed properly. Otherwise, one will experience inconsistent interactivity from those realms and be unable to perform as an environment—or worse, they will be performed, but not as a purposeful consciousness endeavor. Instead, it will be raw and unstructured, lacking conscious leadership and guided only by the domestication occurring outside the consciousness sequence—allowing interactivity to take shape for future conscious leadership.

As development continues, individuals accumulate an interactive base that requires interactivity at a domestic level by means of childhood sentiments. This becomes an experiential signal that occurs independently of conscious conversation, yet becomes a natural state when permitted. These are the conversations that happen organically when space is given—allowing childhood sentiments to achieve conversational maturity with a rounded interactive base.

Without domesticated conversation, one becomes lost to childhood interactions, thereby lacking dynamic exchange with the adult system, reducing them to outbursts of immature emotion with no bearing to the adult structure. Naturally, we seek embodiment and conscious leadership so that infantile sentiment does not remain as such. But proceeding this, it

The Interaction between Structure and Streamline Consciousness

must be contextualized within current values to gain the prerogative for embodiment, which aligns with the existing system. If one gains embodiment purely from infantile sentiment, they establish leadership at an inferior tier of their system—directing consciousness at its lowest level instead of at evocative developmental stages.

If resentment is not domesticated within the interactive domain, it will assume leadership in childhood engagements with parental figures, which hold no place to advanced stages of consciousness. While still being a part of the sequence, it resides at the bottom, giving undue influence to something that could have been raised to a higher position—so that when it reappears, it carries both its foundational aspects and the domesticated maturity needed for final embodiment.

Thus, the domestication of private affairs is a way to address the lowest tiers of the spectrum, so that when embodiment takes place, it does not require the juggling of multiple fragile forms of leadership. Instead, it presents a strong, unified leadership that encompasses all elementary interactive elements.

One might even claim that an individual can domesticate entire interactive experiences without embodiment and still establish a conscious environment for them.

However, one eventually reaches a natural limit to domestication, where all conversations begin to coalesce. If one attempts to continue domestication—such as through therapy—without embodiment, they may lose consciousness leadership at those levels.

For example, if a parental figure continues to require a consciousness attachment in adulthood, the interaction becomes erratic if the sentiment toward that figure is not domesticated. One may fall prey to a conscious environment where political systems take on the role of a parental figure, providing a necessary interactive structure without prior domestication. Once an individual has domesticated their affairs outside the conscious sequence, they will understand the relevance of that parental figure and its connection to other interactive elements. By the time they reach interactive embodiment, they will seek nuanced leadership, not political representation.

Consciousness and Existential Instability: A Comparative Analysis

Comparing the United States and Russia, we see divergent models: one where consciousness is deeply enmeshed in the experience of reality, structuring and giving meaning to its expressions, and another where a commitment to instability—existing in an existential balance where no consciousness is actively attended yet still remains available—results in a detachment from consciousness while still allowing for its ascendancy at a moment's notice.

There are many countries that operate within the existential realm without any particular inference to the consciousness network. These are not considered for this discussion, as they do not possess the ability to ascend to a higher layer of consciousness, even if they desired. They are simply committed to existential instability as their only manner of being, so that it does not cause an uproar in the psyche or disrupt their cultural haven.

The Structure of Consciousness

There is no imaginative expression that would give rise to any transformative abilities.

The United States: Consciousness Enmeshed

The United States represents a consciousness fully absorbed within itself, where nothing exists outside of its own networks of perception and understanding. Every element of existence is processed through structured awareness, where actions, thoughts, and even transgressions must be contextualized and explained within a consciousness framework. There is no room for instability—everything must be positioned within a discourse, whether political, moral, or social.

This explains the endless cycles of ideological confrontation, media spectacle, and public discourse, where even violence is not a remote act but an element of engagement. Even destruction itself becomes part of a system—it is the sinister element of consciousness rather than an instability elsewhere. It is something to be analyzed, interpreted, or even mythologized. This is why manslaughter, crime, and conflict are not merely statistical occurrences but expressive engagements, subject to discussion, entertainment, and even fascination. The depth of this cognizance means that nothing is purely accidental; every event, from a political scandal to an act of violence, must carry significance.

Russia: Existential Instability and Detachment

Russia, by difference, does not engage with its peculiar reality in the same way. It is not an enmeshed consciousness; it is an unstable and detached one, where events do not necessarily integrate into a structured cultural awareness. The experience of existence is transient; where occurrences are not necessarily tied to deeper narratives, instead exist as unconnected phenomena.

There is no inherent fascination with manslaughter or crime because there is no need for such effects to fit within a network of consciousness. Violence, disruption, and change are not necessarily perceived as part of a greater experience but simply as things that happen in isolation—or, more accurately, as manifestations of the nothingness that lies behind consciousness. For them, the act of manslaughter is not seen as a result of something nor as a reflection of its relevant social environment but merely as existence itself, raw and unnegotiable.

This is why we do not see the same compulsive engagement with transgression, nor the same mythologization of crime or violence. Russia moves past such occurrences without necessarily integrating them into its self-perception. This does not mean that Russia lacks depth or complexity, but rather that it operates outside of an enmeshed consciousness system.

However, this very trait—connecting to the instability of existence—is the cause rather than the manifestation of man's nature. Although this may seem like a purely cultural phenomenon, on a psychological level, by committing to remain on the sidelines between adherence and existential instability, individuals remain one-step removed from the homicidal act just the same.

Just as consciousness can compel someone to act on impulse and push their conjectures to extremes—potentially even to the point of homicide—so too, when one disconnects from consciousness at a pathological level and chooses to remain in existential disarray, the consciousness to which they remain tethered will inevitably assert itself. In this way, they have little control over their impulses because they are un-positioned in their existential disarray. They find themselves concerned with a consciousness sentiment precisely because they are, in reality, gaining vitality in the disarray via a consciousness connection.

Mammalian psyches do not experience existential disarray because they are not tethered to a consciousness network. However, it is precisely the significance of consciousness that allows one to remain in that disarray. Yet, this is the very mistake that fuels the homicide this locale: the failure to recognize that remaining in existential instability is merely another manifestation of consciousness. There is no true refuge, for any attempted escape is simply another form of consciousness.

While this is true on some level, one must adhere to their psychological experience and accept that existential disarray is merely the sidelines of consciousness—despite evidence to the contrary. If one does not allow psychological reality to override evidential reality, they will never be able to disengage from consciousness.

On a scientific level, we may say that there exists a realm outside of consciousness that cannot be directly discussed but is instead intuited—not as a *shadow* of consciousness, but as disarray for its own sake. This paradox plays out in the high crime of both countries, as neither fully accepts this complex reality.

One has little control over their impulses if they remain stagnated in disarray, for a mediocre consciousness experience will eventually erupt into action without restraint. After all, in such a moment, they finally receive the vitality they had been lacking. Likewise, when one is deprived of consciousness for prolonged periods, any experience of its substance will be venerated—regardless of its substandard nature or logical contradictions.

This explains how one may fall prey to sexual crime—not out of necessity, but because they have finally found a quantity of consciousness, leading them to assume such to be the only reality worth pursuing, without any diligence to its consequences.

The Interactive Foundations of Consciousness

As previously noted, conscious expansion is not an experienced state, nor is it accessible through taste or any other perceptual senses. The reason for any interaction occurring during times when the senses are unavailable is to allow an individual to retreat into an interactive state, where they may experience this expansion or distribution. The inquiry is most distinguished by its proximity to expansion or wholesome consciousness, both in conceptual and psychical terms, thus aligning closely with consciousness itself. The central locale concerning this thought-process is significant because it departs from consciousness to become a mainstay of any source. Something can only be centered if it has already moved beyond the field of animation; much like a representational figure is no longer considered an individual in the eyes of society.

Since expansion must be experienced in order to serve as a basis for consciousness, this does not imply it is not the true formation of consciousness. Rather, it indicates that the individual parameters inherent in higher life forms are necessary, with consciousness being no exception. Consequently, we must ask where true consciousness resides if central locales themselves represent interactive deviations from its authentic state. One might argue that any interactive deviation—especially regarding the central locale—must remain as arbitrary as possible to avoid disrupting the direct lineage of consciousness.

For this reason, one may develop an acclimatization to the disruptive notion that, because the central locale only postulates a very liminal state of experience without much adherence to innate biological function, it evidences its deviation from real consciousness. This is analogous to a child who perceives the movements of parental figures without much attentiveness to the general experience of the family, suggesting that the child has somehow deviated from the course of the family body. When we acknowledge the true nature of the dynamic, we realize that parental figures do not require much interaction because of their preliminary development in the direction of the family body. Meanwhile, the child requires a full biological attachment, to which the parent only requires arbitrary contact to fulfill the experience of the family body.

The Interactive Mainframe and Consciousness

The very model of the system, as the center, means that anything more than an arbitrary attachment to the central locale will disrupt the attachment to genuine expansion. Still, the experience of any form of consciousness occurs through the interactive mainframe. As one moves closer to the central locale, the interactive mainframe becomes an arbitrary hedge into that material. Thus, a far approximation from the central locale would require a fairly complex interactive mainframe to experience that propagating consciousness. At that distance, one would need a very narrow and distinct contextual basis for the interaction. When the interaction extends beyond that, it would be experiencing an encapsulation of consciousness that is standalone and separate from the central locale.

The necessity for such intervals in which there is an interactive platform for the conscious experience is crucial—not only to sequester timestamps for life experiences but also to provide a haven for influencing future events until the next interactive *platform*. For example, a birthday is an interactive experience that takes the wholesome nature of individual growth and impresses it with a specific time and moment. This serves to separate time periods, such as one year from the next, while also providing a memorial setting from which future material can be extracted.

When things are not sequestered, and years simply pass by, information cannot influence the future because nothing is differentiated, and there is no dynamic interaction between time periods. However, when one differentiates and separates from the locale to be sequestered, it gains the ability to interact with both future and past. This natural celebration of the year allows a single year to interact with another, preventing life from becoming a long continuum of undifferentiated information and experience.

The Second Type of Interactive Locale: Exemplified Interactivity

The second type of interactive locale, namely the locale that provisions exemplified interactivity instead of mediating interactivity, may seem different, nevertheless is only metaphorically reshaped so that the interaction can be successful in a thorough motion—at the cost of presuming the value of being an entirely new entity. Within this locale, it would seem like a setting of demanding interactivity, where one cannot place themselves at the behest of any of its differentiations because each is proposing away from its true value.

Even more so, due to such a multitude of interactivity, there is almost no means to acknowledge that which is directing toward the consciousness continuum and such that is attempting to rebirth the system. By being an exemplified version, one cannot know if it is an interaction of value—meaning that it leads back to the consciousness system in a coherent manner—or if it leads to itself as being merely a substance to stand for itself, threatening to depart from the continuum for a revival of consciousness. A revival of consciousness is problematic because the surrounding environment has not faded into oblivion, so such would only actualize a departure from systemic interaction.

The entity itself does not propose the dichotomy of either direction because it only exemplifies something diverse. One must understand the metaphor to know where the source is derived and where it is not. Similar to the *interactive embodied environment*, where the experience is within a perpetual loop, that certain elements lead to the consciousness continuum, other elements—because of the extensive elaboration of the loop—will, at any given moment, prove to be the portal to the consciousness system to thus provide vitality.

Even if the interactivity is exposed toward a direction that is not meant to be sourced in a continuum, one can ascertain its value accordingly within a consciousness medium. Because it is still an interactive locale—by being the provision of a complete fabrication—it has the benefit that no direction is wrong and, alternatively, no direction is correct. Only through interpretation and contextual basis can we find an interactive direction toward a consciousness medium, despite the intentional realm being arbitrary due to the metaphor itself.

Of course, the natural direction follows a certain exemplified path, but this is only a means to gain vitality for the system. It is by no means the direction an individual must take. One is not required to gain vitality from the continuum by finding the portal itself—the interactive component itself—but rather utilizing any interactivity to expose their internal consciousness. Children, and those not yet exposed to consciousness or lacking the memory traces necessary for such awareness, must progress through the entire system of interactivity—moving from one interaction to the next—until they reach the portal and attain vitality. Worse still, because they do not contain a metric to distinguish, they may assume that any interactive element that is reached is the direction toward material consciousness, only to find that it is merely a revival attempt, which leads to their demise.

We can even define childhood in this manner: a constructed movement between interactivities, where betrayal of reception is instituted with the attempt at another, until one finds a genuine direction toward the consciousness system. Usually, the system itself will highlight certain parts for illumination, but the child may find that these do not lead to cumbersome substance but rather a vitalization in contradiction of the broader system. Some children will find respite in this and will thus reach

The Second Type of Interactive Locale: Exemplified Interactivity

adulthood through the constructed actualization of elements that keep them deeply secluded from accurate consciousness.

There will be interactive elements highlighted either as reminders of a consciousness substance or for another purpose. Whether the substance is part of the sequence, a retrogression, or a revival of consciousness does not matter from the individual's perspective. The interactivity is merely to give an impression of a consciousness system, despite being an interactive locale, so that the interactivity is only an ornament to create the impression of substance. To adhere to that impression can lead either to a true component of the system or to something merely arbitrary, serving the necessity of the current sequence. However, an individual does not concern themselves with the ornament but rather with the system that can be utilized to their advantage.

Reconsidering the Separation of Space

I stand corrected from a previous work, in which we spoke of the impossibility of an interactive domain being sincere in the emanating locale, especially the central locale. Now, the reason for the premise was that, in the structural sense, this seems to be the case: how would one distinguish the specific space with such reliability that a single room would be considered part of the emanating process, and the subsequent would be a comprehensive interactive domain?

The structural location does not give the reserve for such a premise, as if to say that somehow the washroom of a house can be considered a separate entity from the house, despite no vibrant structural separation. Whatever the sentiment of the house, it would be prevalent for the washroom to take upon a similar experience, and to have the experience be different was assumed during our study to be a utopian idea.

However, we must change direction and recognize the possibility, even if, in the structural sense, this may not be the full case. This does require a mental feat alongside the structural sense, which creates a highly formulated definition of space and structure. The washroom is, in fact, separated by its chamber boundaries and doorway, but also in its conceptual inference. What is done within the washroom would dare not be imposed outside of it, and thereby, with both the conceptual and psychological

The Structure of Consciousness

separation in effect, we would only need the individual attention range to mark that distinction. Because of the ease between the change of space from outside the washroom and within, the mental capacity simply considers it to be of the same system, albeit with slight changes.

Yet, with a fairly conceptual separation, where the inside is considered for its physical and conceptual separation, one would be able to experience the washroom as an entity that is completely distinct from the house. The only reason this such is usually not the instance is because one cannot merely alter the entire conceptual framework while entering and exiting rooms and we can imagine the mental exertion for such maintenance.

Instead, we consider it to be a part of the house, thus allowing freedom of movement without the change of conceptual differentiation but with minor deviations that are allotted to the formulation of each room. The cause of which, one does not make use of the house in its potential, but rather as a singular space that has the same possibility in any of its compartments. Is this not the fantasy of a palace, in which it is structurally designed to have the compartments item in a manner where there is compelled separation between spaces, thereby allowing for the entire landscape of manifold conceptual frameworks that offer a unique experience in each individually?

However, if ever having met one who resides in a palace, they will note that it is experienced as the same as any house, because one cannot maintain that change of framework and instead becomes familiar with the space as a singularity. If anyone has experienced distress in a specific room of a house, they will notice that it offers a reality framework that cannot be considered alongside the rest of the house; the room is granted its full scope of solitary structure.

The usual manner in which the palace does take full effect is when there is distinct sociality that maintains the frameworks that pertain to each room, with each quarter given its distinctive recognition amongst the social class, disallowing one to simply connect the rooms and compartments as being a singular structure. Yet, this also has the general deviation where the sociality mechanisms to the benefit of that distinction, and the quarter of a certain regard loses its connection to the familiar aspects of the palace and thus is not considered at all for its unified experience.

The notable quarter where behavior is strictly adhered would also not disseminate its information across the palace. It may be that the quarter can be considered for being a distant terrestrial location in its reciprocity between spaces. Only an individual who adheres to associations of that separation, as would with two fairly distant locations, would attempt a process of allowing reciprocity between them. But in the usual case, the individual will treat them as distinct entities without the possibility of connection.

Inconsistent Interactivity

When interactivity becomes erratic—characterized by an excess of streamlined data tied to specific domesticated processes that correspond to distinct and disconnected helms of consciousness—it reveals a deeper issue. In such cases, we are not merely encountering a conflict of interactivity, but a fundamental conflict of consciousness itself. The interactivity cannot engage with the other to find a consensus because it does not relate to the other. This lack of affiliation leads us back to the conscious conflict between two encapsulations, creating a division.

To illustrate how interactivity cannot relate to each other, it would be as if a child were attempting to listen to an adult's problem and become a friend to that situation. Even more pertinent would be if an adult attempted to alleviate personal resentment toward a child through direct communication. Because of the vast distance of conscious attachments that deal with children and adults, there is little sensibility that interactivity should be regarded with any resilience.

This is why we have mentioned the process of amelioration or therapeutic mending, which integrates interactivity into a cohesive unit of systemic emotional integrity. Although it allows for integration, it does not necessarily lead to mutual understanding. Once the therapeutic process has been undertaken and erratic interactivity is no longer present, the conscious conflict appears to dissolve—not because it is truly resolved, but because it has not ascended to a certain awareness at that moment. Every psyche contains a vast database of conscious conflicts, but these conflicts are not recognized as such until they are granted credence as vital to the present moment.

As a side point, when we find psychological disturbance in populations or individuals, they are not to be considered conflicts for their own sake. Every individual is plagued by conflicts, and that is the normal process of the psyche. It is merely the ascendancy of those conflicts—when they are realized and actualized in the emotional realm—that makes them a pressing matter according to their symptoms.

When interactivity is settled, one can retrace or reactivate a new form of consciousness. Alternatively, one can enter into communion with

The Structure of Consciousness

newfound experiences of consciousness and its subtle interactivity. However, if erratic interactivity and conscious conflicts persist, then entering into a new conscious realm will be overlaid with these mature conscious layers, so that the new layer is simply a reactivation of the former.

When this happens—such as when one is enduring interactivity based on an infantile stage that has not been ameliorated, and thus there is a conscious leadership based on the development of that particular period in time—then upon entering the communal space of current consciousness, it will only serve to re-emphasize that infantile layer and its consciousness leadership. In effect, one existentially becomes akin to a child. It is as though one is actualizing through the prism of an earlier stage of development.

It is also the case that this prior frame is brought into the reception of new consciousness. If an individual reaches a higher level of interaction with real-time consciousness, the entire realm receptive to it will be influenced by that unresolved element. This is why we hold a higher standard for political office and its representations, especially regarding moral virtue—because there is an association between the political realm and consciousness.

Moral degeneracy does more than merely tarnish a candidate's stature—it fundamentally undermines their appropriateness for political office. What is happening, rather, is the infusion of sentiment into a consciousness system at an extraordinary level, where an infantile attachment becomes framed within the perceived innocence and perfection of current consciousness development. Of course, this is merely an expectation—a symbolic projection—of what political office represents. Politicians are not necessarily contributing anything directly to the consciousness realm, as the political realm exists separately and largely functions as a buffer. However, the public continues to perceive such as a reflection of how consciousness systems operate.

This phenomenon becomes evident when someone experiences a psychological breakdown in a high-consciousness environment—where the crowd or collective sociality internalizes the experience. A baby on a train, for instance, in a state of discomfort, becomes existentially disturbing to strangers because its infantile layer of consciousness is imposed onto the collective. Even though the baby is simply expressing its natural state—not regressing to a prior one—the perception that its distress signals a regression makes it seem like a disruption to the social sphere.

The concern is not just for the baby's discomfort—for the baby is, after all, a stranger—but for what the baby represents: a disruption of consciousness through the expression of erratic interactivity, embodied in the act of crying. Crying emerges from a clash between longstanding consciousness sentiments and their fragmented components. As a result, the entire collective is exposed to this disruption. It is not merely perceived as an external event; rather, the collective is fundamentally altered through the reception of that consciousness.

The Encapsulation of Consciousness and Interactivity

There is always an encapsulation of interactivity accompanying any conscious experience—remnants of elementary forms of consciousness that have ascended into the attention sphere, influencing and directing new conscious experiences. This is, in fact, the nature of consciousness itself: one may rise from a prior layer to engage more fundamentally in a genuine, real-time state. Whatever role elementary consciousness plays, it does not inherently involve direct, present-moment perceptual experience.

As Edelman notes, "misfunctioning of the value-category memory or imbalances in connections [value-category being the apprehension of the consciousness core, and imbalances referring to the lack of stimulation in the core's permeation] to the key reentrant paths for primary consciousness would [I would argue 'can'] lead to a perceptually driven but incoherent set of responses [responses that become incoherent, as the new form is not enjoyed as a novel model but forced to function as a reactionary extension of the elementary one]" (Edelman, 1989, p. 214).[10]

The psyche is most attentive to the perceptual domain, which serves as the clearest expression of its internal operations. Even a schizophrenic must, at some level, submit to this domain in order to sustain the image-like quality that perception provides—never truly able to award more stature to any other domain.

Beyond perception, however, there exists a realism intrinsic to the present moment—one neither burdened by memory nor wholly constructed from prior structures. Whatever information emerges in the immediacy is closest to the true nature of universal consciousness and the continuity of civilization. A person who operates from a developed, memory-based layer

---

[10] Edelman, G.M., *The Remembered Present: A Biological Theory of Consciousness* (1989).

is often granted access to a more permeable and expanded state of awareness. The foundational layer is thereby revisited, altered, and redefined within this new experience—transformed to the point that it may be seen as something new. Yet this same process—wherein the elementary layer acts as a prerequisite—can also become its limitation, particularly when interactivity has not been sufficiently engaged.

Every primary form of consciousness has an associated interactivity, or at least distilled elements of it, that constitute its form. There is some flexibility in how we define and engage with this interactivity—through various modalities and directions. Still, a core always remains, bottled with the potential for interaction until an active process catalyzes it. This is why theoretical frameworks, institutions, locales, and even entire nations that organize such engagements are so vital. Theoretical frameworks offer a competent means of addressing an overloaded consciousness core by systematically deconstructing its elements through theory and abstraction until the core's vitality is dissipated and no longer operates as a nuclear-activated force.

When an activated core attempts to participate in a new, current conscious experience, one is often compelled to rely on the elementary version for grounding—while drawing from a more evolved consciousness layer for continuity. This happens because the core, undomesticated and unanchored, does not know where else to go. It has entered the psyche's attention sphere without direction.

Edelman elaborates on this issue when discussing the stability of memory re-categorization: *"By means of reentrant signaling, different maps separately receiving signals for features or for correlations of features could be connected in time, space, and neural properties and be altered as a result of correlated synaptic changes"* (Edelman, 1989, p. 156).[11]

This constant reorganization keeps consciousness dynamic, yet it also risks fragmentation when interactivity is poorly structured. Correlation, as noted, is key—and correlation can only occur when interactivity or domestication has been properly established. An activated core, in isolation, resists correlation, as it is complete unto itself but lacks relationality to any new model or set of ideas. Ideation allows these distinctions to be realized and enables correlation with the onset of a new consciousness model—

---

[11] Ibid.

Reconsidering the Separation of Space

much like a structural disintegration that has already processed its parts and can thus reorganize into a new, coherent form.

In this sense, a functional theoretical framework becomes a container for the elementary core. It remains vitalized by its intellectual structure, even as the original core dissipates. This is the framework that can then correlate with the formation of a new consciousness model.

This last point is crucial: if an activated core once existed but time has rendered it dormant, then a new conscious experience will not integrate with that elementary state. This is observable, for instance, in childhood, where many activated cores exist—each lacking the interactivity necessary to bring them fully into presence. And because they never enter the attention sphere in an evocative manner, it is as if they were never there at all.

www.ingramcontent.com/pod-product-compliance
Lightning Source LLC
LaVergne TN
LVHW012045070526
838202LV00056B/5601